THE BOOK OF LOVE

by rob and jacq

-AUTHORS OF "THE LETTERS OF GRATITUDE"

IN DEDICATION TO...

For those who are in love, may it continue to flourish.

For those who have lost love, may it find you once again.

For those who have been hurt by love, may love heal you.

For those who pretend to be in love, may the truth escape you.

For those who fear love, may it be love that sets you free.

For those of who hide love, may you find the courage to share it.

For those who speak of love, may you act on what presides within.

For those who cannot accept love, may you learn to embrace it.

For those who silence words of love, may you hear their voices.

For those who love others more than self, may you love yourself most.

For those who use the word love sparingly, may you give it freely.

For those who reserve love to an exclusive few, may you be more inclusive.

For those who love one, may you love all.

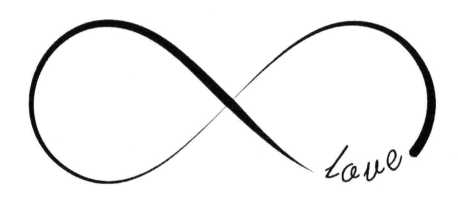

ACKNOWLEDGEMENTS

This book would have been a slow creation had it not been for our contributors. Your voices and courageous stories inspired us to pursue this project with a fiery passion. It is with immense LOVE and gratitude that we thank ALL of the wise people who have contributed to this publication. Thank you for believing in us and our vision.

It is with our deepest love that we give thanks to our family members who honor and celebrate our authenticity and unconventional journey. Your belief and support enhances our happiness beyond measure. Without any of you, our meaning of love just wouldn't be the same. Thank you.

This book was written with love in our hearts to our supporters. Without your unwavering support, our purpose wouldn't have been so clear.

Love:

Origin: Old English *lufu;* akin to Old High German *luba* love, Old English *lēof* dear, Latin *lubēre, libēre* to please.

Transitive Verb: Must have action and a recipient of that action.

i)   To hold dear to your heart while allowing to be held dear.
ii) To thrive and encouraging others to flourish.
iii) To offer affection and feeling the affection given.
iv) To desire and allowing yourself be desired.
v)   To give unselfishly and allowing others to put you first.
vi) To give a lover devotion and feeling their devotion.
vii) To treasure and to be treasured.

FORWARD

LOVE is something that too often we reserve. We hold it close to our being and share it with only a select few. We quantify and qualify why and who we offer our love to, as though our emotions and actions need justification. We judge others up against some imaginary checklist and give our love to only those who are deserving. We offer our love sparingly as though it is a resource that someday may deplete and cease to exist. We dangle and twist it in ways where it is no longer recognizable. We use it as a guise to hide and bandage our truth. It is spoken, heard and acted upon too infrequently. When we hear about loving self, it seems all too new age and mystical. When we hear about romance, too often it is in reference to films and not our lives. Somewhere along the way, the purity and connectivity between love and the universe has been lost.

This BOOK is not only a beginning, it is a calling. It is our universal call to rectify our connection with love. We invite you to fall in love with yourself, give your love to the world, and attract more love into your life.

This is not a passive read, for love does not stand still. This book invites you to read, journal, dream, act, and create more love in your life and the world around you. *The Book of Love* will leave you feeling creative, courageous, inspired, amused, spontaneous, reflective, giving, uplifted and truly emanating love from within. It is for YOUR whole being. It is for ALL beings. The words and actions before you are not daunting, for truth be told love is the easiest gift we can give ourselves and the world around us.

For, THIS is the era of LOVE.

Love
is more than an
emotional state
of being,
it is the sum
of actions
created because
of it...

CONTENTS:

HOW TO USE THE BOOK OF LOVE:

This book was created to inspire change. If we truly want to see more love in the world, then it is up to all of us to be the solution.

The Book of Love will always be free of charge to those who want it. There are zero limitations on those who deserve love in their life and this book reflects that. Help us spread the love by passing it on.

Tell friends and loved ones that the digital version *The Book of Love* is free! (TheLettersofGratitude.com or scan the QR CODE below). All of the interactive pages are available for you to print at home so that if you wish to, you can recycle your physical book by passing it on, donating it, or leaving it in a random place for a stranger to find. Keep the book and work directly in it. Scribble, scribe, and tear this book apart. The choice is yours.

This journey is about you. It is about creating more love within yourself and the world around you.

For us, Love begins with self and this is reflected in the sequence of the book, but it is up to you. Read and work through the book front to back. Start with the end and work to the front. Meander randomly throughout and choose what calls you. Use it as: a doorstop, a paperweight, a fire -starter, an awkward Frisbee, a fan, toilet paper, origami paper, or of course, as a book. The decisions are yours.

Just as there are no rules for LOVE, there are no rules here.

Enjoy your journey!

With LOVE & Gratitude,
Rob and Jacq

SELF-LOVE:

REGARD FOR ONE'S

OWN WELL BEING

AND HAPPINESS.

Adopt Loving Eyes

Our relationship with mirrors and photographs reveals something deeper about the way we view ourselves. Most of us can safely say that we either love, or criticize our reflection. Sadly, many of us can most relate to the latter.

Photos: If you are a cringer, a compulsive editor, or you fanatically delete… this one is for you.

Mirrors: If you are an avoider, if you glance only in short intervals, or if you only use them when shaving or applying creams/make-up… this one is for you.

Take the Reflection Test: Approximately 30 minutes

PART I

What you will need:

- Use a room with a full length mirror that you can have to yourself for at least 30 minutes.
- Cut out and bring the interactive page, one blank sheet of paper, a pen/pencil of your choosing, and your honesty.
- A timer (or do your best to follow the suggested times).

Instructions:

1) Undress.
2) Set your timer to 1 minute. This will feel like a long time, but take the 1 minute to look at you entire being and look closely. Take heed of the thoughts that enter your mind.
3) Take as much time as you need to record all of the thoughts that entered into your mind onto the blank sheet of paper.
4) Use the diagram as a guide. Look at each listed item. In turn, spend at least one minute looking at that particular facet of your body and then at least one minute recording.
5) Once completed, clothe yourself and go to part II when you are ready.

Part II:

1) Review your diagram and notes. Do you want to improve the way you look at yourself? Go to the next step. If you don't, skip the rest of the exercise.
2) Allow that to become a part of your past.
3) Tape the mantras (reverse side of the diagram) to your mirror.
4) Commit to reading them in the mirror for one week.

Part III:

1) Repeat part one, filling in the after section

Part IV:

If you completed this challenge with sincerity, you will have observed change. Keep the mantras within your mind as you move forward.

before

your face

your arms

your chest

your stomach

your legs

after

your face

your arms

your chest

your stomach

your legs

7 MANTRAS FOR 7 DAYS
read with love and sincerity

I.   I LOVE MY EYES. They are unique and special to me. I am grateful that they allow me to see all of the beauty and abundance in the world.

II.   I LOVE MY FACE. It reveals my history with the world and a lifetime of happiness. I am grateful that it reminds me of all of the laughter I have had.

III.   I LOVE MY SMILE. It allows me to share my joy with the world. I am grateful for the memories I have and the smiles that are yet to come.

IV.   I LOVE MY ARMS. They allow me to embrace all of those I love. I am grateful for all that they allow me to do.

V.   I LOVE MY CHEST. My chest is the keeper of my heart and the holder of my breath. I am grateful for the love and life within.

VI.   I LOVE MY STOMACH. It stores my nourishment within. I am grateful for the life it gives and for the beauty of my belly.

VII.   I LOVE MY LEGS. They enable me to go where I am celebrated. I am grateful for my mobility and the journey that is before me.

FILL IN ONE HEART ♥ AFTER EACH DAY

If you
change
the way
you look
at
things,
the things
you look
like
change.
-Wayne Dyer

list 6 things you have always wanted to do, but haven't had THE COURAGE TO TRY:

IT IS TIME 🕐 TO STEP 👣 OUT OF YOUR COMFORT ZONE

INSTRUCTIONS: Roll one dice, or use the scan me code below for electronic dice. The number you have randomly rolled corresponds with the item you recorded on page 18. Here is your "step outside of your comfort zone" challenge!

I Rolled #
My Challenge is

What:
When:
With Who:
Cost:
Feeling:

SCAN ME

19

WRITE, OR DRAW THE DETAILS OF YOUR EXPERIENCE.

what did you love about it?

CONGRATULATIONS FOR LOVING YOURSELF IN A WAY THAT YOU ARE ABLE TO EMBRACE NEW EXPERIENCES

TREAT YOURSELF TO A ZOMBIE DAY

What you will need:

An entire day to yourself...

Instructions:

Do Nothing

Think Nothing.

NO GUILT!

We all have those days where we feel like doing absolutely nothing. The next time you feel that way and can put aside your obligations, take a ZOMBIE DAY! Recharge your batteries with guilt-free REST and RELAXATION. Rejuvenate your mind, body and soul. Every once in a while, this is exactly what you need.

RECORD YOUR RECHARGE DAYS:

HONOR YOUR INNER GUIDE

"My stomach twisted in knots. Everything inside of me told me not to get into the car, but I did anyways. I was drugged and was left with a 12 hour window with no memory. At the age of 15, I learned the hard lesson that I should always listen to my inner guide."

Hindsight is an enlightening gaze that can help us evolve into our best version of self. Regret is useless. It is the lessons within our experiences that are of life-changing value. One of the biggest lessons we have learned is to listen to the voice within. When we are youngsters, many of us are taught to "follow our gut", yet so many of us deafen and defy this voice. We have all been guilty of seeking outside advice when we truly know *our* right answer. We seek affirmation that our truth is "right", even when we know it is correct all along. Listening to our inner voice can nudge us in exactly the right place at the right time. Honoring our inner guide is a cornerstone for loving self.

10 WAYS TO HONOR YOUR INNER GUIDE:

- *love* **Incorporate meditation into your life**. When your mind is clear it creates a space for intuition to speak. Be patient with your practice and be gentle on yourself.
- *love* **Silence**. Get comfortable in whatever way you choose (lying in a bath, sitting in the garden, or a beach etc.) What thoughts come to your mind? What is the significance?
- *love* **Write**. Practice writing "stream of consciousness" style. This is when you write continuously without regard for what and how you are writing. You simply let it flow out. This can often lead to moments of clarity.
- *love* **Trust**. Listening is the first component and the second is trusting. This may be challenging for you in the moment. One good reminder is to take note when you second guess your judgement. Try trusting your initial inclination over your analytical judgements.

- *love* **Avoid seeking and offering advice**. Pay close attention when you ask others advice. Are you looking to affirm something intuitive?

- *love* **Connect with nature with no distractions** (such as music, or company). Go for a solo walk anywhere where you can be alone with the natural world. For many, this is a bridge to their inner voice.

- *love* **Have the courage to say yes, no, or I am unsure**. We often commit to particular experiences, or follow certain paths because we feel like we are obliged, or because we are concerned with the judgement/opinions of others. Love yourself in a way that you honor your truth and the voice of your inner guide MORE than the chatter of your surroundings.

- *love* **Practice Gratitude**. Spend some time appreciating what you *really* appreciate and not what you *should* appreciate. When you take time in the morning and the evening to be thankful, you will be surprised at what other thoughts "pop" in. Pay attention to what arises!

- *love* **Be flexible.** Not all of us are spontaneous, so for all of the planners this one is for you. Keep an open mind when it comes to adjusting your plans. Sometimes your intuition will nudge you in a way that opposes your plans.

- *love* **Differentiate between wanting to do something and being drawn somewhere**. Acknowledge that intuition is not always logical. Sometimes you may be magnetized to doing something, or going somewhere you have never had the desire to. While other times, you will feel a repulsion to doing something that you normally would like. Our inner guide often opposes the persona we have created for ourselves.

- *love* **Observe coincidences, nudges and hints from the universe**. Acknowledge the guidance you have been given. You will feel your energy rise, or decrease around people. What does this mean to you? Use the journal page to make a record and honor your inner guide.

Your Inner Guide

JOURNAL WHAT YOUR INNER GUIDE HAS TAUGHT YOU.

When you listen
to what
presides,
within
a remarkable
voice speaks.
The real magic
occurs when
you listen.
-The Letters of Gratitude

GO ON A DATE WITH...
YOURSELF

Taking yourself on a date is one of the most empowering and revealing acts of self-love. If you feel inclined to skip this exercise, what does that reveal about the way you love yourself? When our actions meet our inner dialogue, an incredible shift occurs within ourselves and the world around us. If our language and life are in contradiction, we feel confused, chaotic, and drained. Yet, if they are synchronism, we feel inspired, peaceful, and energized. Our loving words and thoughts are powerful beyond measure, but it is only when we combine it with our lifestyle that a true spiritual evolution occurs.

- ♡ WHO: Just you!
- ♡ WHAT: Take the time to chime into your needs and desires. Ask yourself, what do I need right now? What do I want right now? What am I really passionate about? Use the ideas page to gather inspiration.
- ♡ WHEN: Once a week and for a minimum of one hour. Love yourself in a way that you are able to prioritize your well-being.
- ♡ WHERE: Choose a new location each week. Try your best to mix it up.
- ♡ WHY: Because you LOVE yourself.

date ideas:

Need Relaxation? Go for a massage, treat yourself to a solo dinner out, have a candlelit bath, choose your favorite form of pampering and indulge.

Need Energy? Exercise, go dancing, take a dance class, go for a scenic drive or bike ride and crank your favorite music.

Need Peace? Meditation (page 92), nature walk, listen to classical music and write.

Need Spontaneity? Pick a number between 1 and 100. After you have chosen, go to page 29 and do the corresponding exercise. Or, check out the article on page 44

Need Creativity? Check out the list on page 29.

Need Laughter? Go to a comedy show, take yourself out to a funny movie, read jokes.

PLAN YOUR DATES:

Week 1
What:
When:
Where:

Week 2
What:
When:
Where:

Week 3
What:
When:
Where:

Week 4
What:
When:
Where:

we are all
CREATIVE BEINGS!

it is amazing how

the process

of creation energizes

AND LIFTS YOUR SOUL.

100 IDEAS TO FUEL YOUR CREATIVE SOUL

choose something and have fun

1. **Draw a flipbook cartoon (flip through page 175- 215)**
2. Write a poem (check out the QR Code Below for Writing Starters)
3. Write a book
4. Write a short story
5. Make a flower arrangement
6. Watch drawing tutorials and follow along
7. Get a canvas and paint
8. Sculpt with clay, or weld a sculpture
9. Knit
10. Crotchet
11. Embroider, or weave
12. Make jewelry
13. Cook without a recipe and have someone else choose your main ingredient
14. Redecorate a room in your house
15. Pick flowers
16. Plant flowers
17. Make candles (with surprises inside)
18. Bake
19. Break old pottery and make a mosaic
20. Origami

21. Design and Sew an Outfit
22. Revamp something old into something new
23. Make a chalkboard wall
24. Bake something you have always wanted to try
25. Go for a beach walk to collect shells, sand, or rocks and make something
26. See if you can come up for a NEW use for mason jars (good luck)
27. Invent something
28. Play a musical instrument
29. Compose a song
30. Write a play
31. Upholster something
32. Build a website
33. Start a blog
34. Take the time to create a new hairstyle
35. Write a letter
36. Start a gratitude journal (write or draw)
37. Build a piece of furniture
38. Create gadgets to solve your household frustrations.
39. Make a Zen garden
40. Concoct your own olive oil infusions
41. Make soap
42. Recreate the food in fairytales/nursery rhymes (green eggs and ham)
43. Draw an animated sketchbook
44. Make a scrapbook
45. Invent smoothie/juice recipes
46. Recreate your favorite recipe in a different style (Mediterranean, Thai, Chinese, etc.)
47. Take dance classes, or learn a dance from YouTube
48. Make a personalized sugar scrub (recipe on page 120)
49. Make playlists of your favorite songs and categorize them by mood or activity (exercise music, cooking music, get happy playlist etc.)
50. Write a Song (put it online)

51. Teach someone something creative you already do
52. Take photos, develop them and create something from them
53. Create and host a scavenger hunt in your city
54. Invent your own exercise system
55. Create a hula hoop routine to unexpected music
56. Try belly dancing
57. Write and preform a rap song
58. Make your own perfume/cologne
59. Choreograph a flash mob
60. Make a dream catcher
61. Calligraphy
62. Carve something
63. Make a lampshade
64. Design the architecture or interior of your dream house
65. Learn photo editing with Photoshop
66. Make stepping stones for your garden
67. Plan and execute an event/party with a fun theme
68. Learn to sing a song in a new language
69. Take acting classes, or play around at home by watching your favorite movies and emulating the screen
70. Design a tattoo
71. Design and make an app
72. Write imaginative horoscopes for friends and family
73. Play in your closet and make up new outfits
74. Design an awesome outfit entirely made up from thrift store finds
75. Dig out your boxed photos and make collages
76. Make a photo video with music
77. Create a photo/picture frame with reclaimed wood
78. Choreograph and interpretive dance on the topic of love
79. Write and send a message in a bottle to your future self
80. Plan in detail a one month dream vacation on a budget
81. Lip sync a song and post it for fun

82. Create a time capsule for someone to find
83. Invent your own signature drink and come up with a fun name
84. Design your own t-shirt (check out Tee Springs)
85. Draw a cartoon
86. Play Charades
87. Host a scary story night where everyone has to tell them improve style
88. Make a beautiful fishpond
89. Learn the yoyo and make a routine
90. Make wind chimes with recycled items
91. Create a henna design
92. Make an infographic for something you are passionate about
93. Meditate to spark a creative idea
94. Write a recipe book based on all of your own concoctions
95. Make a birdhouse
96. Design a costume
97. Host a tapas night with a food and costume theme
98. Host a martini night where everyone brings one bottle. Have fun creating new concoctions for all of your friends to try.
99. Decorate cakes/cupcakes or host a contest with a random theme
100. Write a list of 100 creative things that you can do

SCAN ME

We decided to move across the world and give up our careers: I remember some of it with intense and vivid recollection, but for the most part is was a blur. It began with a *"what if"* conversation and ended with the plan to move across the world. Great, we have a plan! That's unusual. In the one year between the imaginary and the reality of making it happen, I wasn't able to grasp all of logistics until they were staring me head on. How do you start over? What do you need to do? Isn't there a book for this? Why would you walk away from your career? Have you really thought this through? NO! How will you make a living? Oh $%! I should have thought of that! Are you insane? Maybe… When do you *break* the news? I need to fit my entire life in a backpack! What?! No Storage???

AND how do you part with your beloved…shoes?

I won't bother with all the detail, but for the most part it was smooth-ish sailing. Of all the responses, through the challenges and triumphs, I have to admit that I am most haunted by the way I reacted to my shoes. Embarrassingly saying, "See you in a year" to friends seemed easy compared with saying the finite goodbye to the stilettos. I remember during one of our live radio interviews this being the brunt of a joke and I too have to admit that it was truly absurd.

The hard hitting truth of all of this was, that *is* who I was. I can't change it. At that time, that *was* important to me. Although an uncomfortable statement now, they *were* worth all those tears (yes, there were many). Beneath it all, I loved my shoes.

WHEN I DUG DEEPER, I REALIZED THIS:

- I worked a part time job to supplement my full time career, to subsidize my shopping. That's in excess of 1,000 extra hours of work per year!
- I traded sleep, relaxation, pursuing other passions, time with family, and time with friends for STUFF.
- New things were an emotional Band-Aid.
- My shoe closet was cluttered and it stressed me out (yes, they had a separate closet).
- I never had enough money, but I didn't have any more hours in the day.

- ♡ My shoes could have easily been exchanged for other things of little *value*.
- ♡ I was not an anomaly.
- ♡ Life experience and self-love were not a priority.
- ♡ *They* filled a void.
- ♡ Apparently, I am not tall.
- ♡ Flat shoes are comfortable!
- ♡ Despite my facets of happiness, I was unhappy.
- ♡ Those countless tears were worth the lesson.

The irony of all of it was we went to Thailand to start our journey of travel and gratitude. This was a spiritual journey that had nothing to do with what I defined with "looking nice". Besides, the pavements are uneven and my shoes would not only have been uncomfortable, but also potentially dangerous (no joke). True to all *so-called* sacrifices, the lesson was and still is far bigger than the loss.

Try This:

Fit your entire life in a backpack, or suitcase and then ask yourself, "What is really important?"

Ask Yourself This with Honesty:

- ♡ Even if it is a wild dream, what do you REALLY want in life?
- ♡ Where does your money go?
- ♡ Where is the excess?
- ♡ What can you declutter?
- ♡ What do you need?
- ♡ What can you sell?
- ♡ What can you donate?
- ♡ What will you give up to finance your dreams?
- ♡ What do you want?
- ♡ Are you worth it?

TO LIVE FULLY,
WE MUST LEARN
to use things
and love people,
AND NOT
love things
and use people.
—john powell

AS WE GROW INTO OUR WISDOM, IT IS IMPORTANT TO ACKNOWLEDGE WHO WE ARE, INSTEAD OF LIVING IN THE REFLECTION OF WHO WE WERE.

LOVE AND RESPECT THE EVOLUTION OF SELF

Who we are, what we want, what we believe in, and what we are passionate about is constantly evolving. New experiences teach us, transform the color of our horizons and our perceptions shift. As we grow into our wisdom, it is important to acknowledge and honor *who we are*, instead of living in the reflection of *who we were*.

Thoughts to Keep in Mind:

- Be willing to give up on old dreams. The dreams that we had are not necessarily relevant to who we are. Our "bucket-lists" should be constantly shifting as we grow. As we let go of old dreams, we can add new ones that are more reflective of who we are.
- Adapt old adages to match your inner evolution.
- Take the time to honor what you are really passionate about in this moment.
- ~~Try~~ Chase new experiences.
- Embrace the stumbles and falls as teaching tools. This is a foundation of growth.
- Share your evolution with others without seeking advice.
- Get out of your past by respecting who you are now.
- Give yourself a makeover to honor your change.
- Check in with yourself often.

10 Questions to Consider when Recording your Evolution on the Brainstorm Pages:

1) Who did/do I love and why?
2) What did/do I believe in?
3) What did/do I want for my future?
4) What was/is the most important goal for me?
5) What was/is my emotional priority?
6) How did/do I define happiness?
7) How did/do I demonstrate self-love?
8) How did/do I define friendship?
9) What was/am I passionate about?
10) What did/do I dream of?

WHO WAS I FIVE YEARS AGO?

WHO AM I IN THIS MOMENT?

gratitude
is not just
A WORD,
IT IS OUR WAY
of life.

Set and Live by your Emotional Intentions

Living with intention is to live by the priorities that YOU set. It is choosing a daily, monthly, or life commitment and living accordingly. This type of *lifestyle* differs from those who live *unintentionally* because it is driven by emotional needs, rather than being focused on surface desires. Those who do not live intentionally move robotically through life without truly reflecting on *why*. For example, "Today I have to work, pick up groceries, make dinner, catch my favorite show, and get to bed." Although there is absolutely nothing wrong with this life, it can be enhanced with the addition of an emotional intention.

Setting and living our emotional intentions gives purpose, goals, increases happiness, and helps to make clear decisions. Four years ago, our emotional intention was to live with gratitude. It began with 30 days of appreciation and led to one of our most drastic life changes. The decision to live with the intention of appreciation for everything naturally caused the re-evaluation of all facets of our life. Once again, we have added living with love to our intentions. Setting an intention alters our way of seeing, being, and living.

How to Set an Emotional Intention:

- *love* → Choose your emotional goal. In this moment, do you want happiness? Gratitude? Love? Peace? Passion? Empathy? Etc.
- *love* → Use the journal page to write it down in the form of a mantra. For example, I live with love for all beings and experiences.
- *love* → Keep your mantra in your mind. Think about it as you wake and navigate through your day.
- *love* → When you are feeling indecisive, think about your mantra.
- *love* → Be kind to yourself when you lose focus. Acknowledge when you feel as though you weren't living by your intention, and make the necessary shift.
- *love* → Be reflective. Use the journal page to make note of positive shifts that you notice.
- *love* → When you are ready, begin the process of re-evaluation. What/who no longer fits into your way of life?
- *love* → Act. If your intention is to live with happiness, you will likely need to make changes in your lifestyle.
- *love* → Congratulate yourself. Change takes courage!

MY EMOTIONAL INTENTIONS AND MANTRAS TO LIVE BY:

Every one
of my decisions is balanced
by the weight
of gratitude,
just as every thought
is coloured with
the intensity,
passion and generosity
of LOVE.

SPONTANEITY FOR SELF-LOVE

If monotony is the plague to the soul, than spontaneity is the fountain of youth. Regardless of your schedule, you can always mix up your routine and build more excitement into your life. Being spontaneous can be a challenge for many people, especially for the *planners,* but sometimes all it takes is little a nudge to get the ball rolling.

a few thoughts to consider:

- ♡ Rethink your routine in a way that will allow for the unexpected. Do you normally cook dinner alone? Or does someone else in the house? Mix it up! Have a cook-off one night. Who can make the best_____? Randomly go out for dinner based on a "phone of friend" suggestion, or write down 6 places and roll one dice.
- ♡ For those who are really busy, or have a hard time incorporating this, build spontaneous time into your schedule. Try giving yourself one day a week, or a month to do something out of the blue. Go for a road trip and let the radio guide you. At the beginning of a new song, for a female artist turn right and for a male turn left. Create whatever rules you want to help build excitement.
- ♡ Invite friends, or family to participate and challenge them to be more spontaneous too!
- ♡ Make the most out of your free time and don't exclude *work nights!* You don't need an entire day or two, Mondays can be awesome too.
- ♡ Consider doing something silly! Check out the list on page 67.
- ♡ Follow your inclinations. Do you ever catch yourself saying, "I wish I could…" Often, we can do exactly what we want. Remember, whatever your norm, that is what you have created.
- ♡ Lastly, if you want to be free-spirited, give yourself permission to be. Sometimes, our lives resemble what it *should* look like, rather than what we really *want,* or *need* it to be. Being spontaneous is not irresponsible, it is imperative to loving ourselves.

SPIN THE SPONTANEITY WHEEL

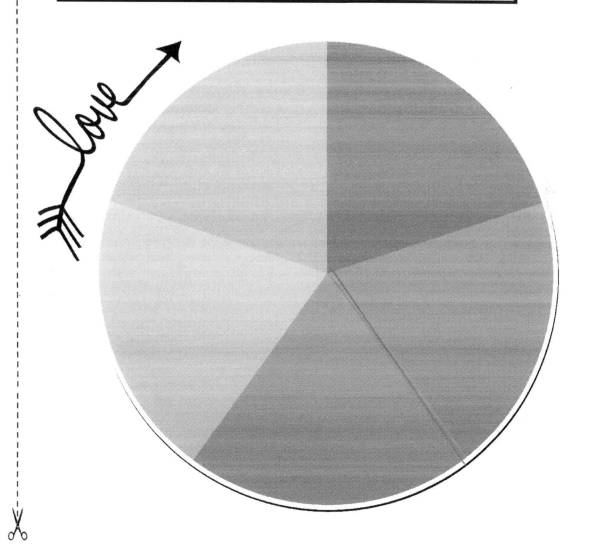

It is within
the unexpected that
our pulse pushes
a little faster,
our smile grows
a little bigger,
and our hearts feel
a whole lot fuller.

One of the joys of childhood is the unadulterated imagination and dreams. We do not categorize as realistic, illogical, or impractical. Our wildest dreams live within our minds and *everything* seems possible. As we grow and experience life, social norms often cloud our dreams. We begin to label them in terms of plausibility and suddenly following our heart becomes an unworthy gamble. And too often, we live the lives that appear *normal*, when what we truly want dwells in the same spirit as fairytales and Hollywood films. Our dreams get scribed on a list that we will look at when we have the *time,* or the *financial resources* to make it happen.

CONSIDER THIS:

- ♡ Why is it that we consider working a career we hate as *safe* when it truly is unsafe to our psyche?
- ♡ Why is it that our path looks uncannily close to the people we know, yet when all we yearn to be unique?
- ♡ Why is it that we wait until retirement to start living?
- ♡ Why is it that we plan every last detail knowing that it won't work that way, yet we feel disappointed?
- ♡ Why is it that we use our age as an excuse to not do something, when it really should urge us to begin?
- ♡ Why is it that we put more value on our material goods than our experiences?
- ♡ Why do we consider it a *risk* to follow our dreams when the only real risk is never chasing them?

When we truly start to examine our lives, it often doesn't make sense. We dare you to start dreaming and start dreaming big! Use the journal page to reconnect with what you TRULY want.

DESCRIBE YOUR DREAM LIFE ✏️
BE WILD & IMAGINATIVE!

IT IS NEVER TOO LATE TO be what you might have been.

— George Eliot —

Dreaming without action is like living without breathing. Use these pages to plot your plan. Break down the details: include specific dates and exactly what you need to do to make it happen! Use the logistics you create as YOUR PLAN.

SELF-LOVE AND CHASING OUR DREAMS ARE AS

inseparable as the sea is to sand.

When what we dream and do
are a mirror of the other, we become ourselves.

THE THINGS THAT

YOU ARE PASSIONATE

ABOUT ARE NOT RANDOM,

THEY ARE YOUR

CALLING.

-FABIENNE FREDRICKSON

pursue your PASSIONS

Pursuing passions is to love the soul. Sometimes life gets busy and our passions get put to the wayside. They become unwarranted, forgotten, time-consumers, childish, irrelevant, or are undiscovered. Everything else takes precedence and that which energized us, vanishes out of our existence. Some of us are taught that our passions are not purposeful, or are judged useless because they don't equate with a dollar value. Passions get confused with goals and suddenly people are left retired, bored and lifeless. People without passions soak up drama, create it, are frustrated, and gossip without truly understanding why. This so-called excitement becomes a temporary solution for the fiery roar of passion. Yet, there are a lucky few whose passions and careers intertwine. Our passions are our purpose and to negate them is suffocating to our soul.

When we take the time to prioritize our passions, our life transforms. We emanate love because we have taken the time to love ourselves. We feel nourished, grateful, peaceful, purposeful, energized and excited. Truly, those who take this time to pursue their passions can not only love better, they live better too.

Enough said, let's get to it!

discover new passions:

If you already have an exhaustive list, or are happy with your passions, move on to the next section. For those of you who want to discover your passions, or find new ones, this section is for you!

This is about you and honoring your self-love through action.

a few reminders:

- → Be gentle on yourself.
- → Allow yourself to make mistakes because you will.
- → Don't create expectations.
- → Don't compare yourself.
- → Allow yourself to be a beginner and grow.
- → It is not about being *good,* it is about being yourself.
- → Be honest with yourself.
- → Share what you are doing without asking people what they think.
- → Be willing to try things outside of your comfort zone.
- → Don't judge yourself based on what you are drawn to.
- → It is okay if your passion contrasts what is typical for you.
- → Drop preconceived gender *norms.*
- → Be open to *odd* (for example, I recently realized I am passionate about brainstorming! Go figure).

Questions to Assist you in Uncovering your Passions:

1. **GO BACK IN TIME (As a child & adolescent):**
   - ♡ What were your favorite things to do?

   - ♡ What did you beg you parents to let you stay up late to do?

   - ♡ What were not allowed to do, but really wanted to?

♡ What could you do for hours without noticing time had slipped away?

♡ What were you doing when you were left alone?

♡ What were you doing that gave you the most energy?

♡ What did you consider fun?

♡ What was your favorite subject/elective/activity at school?

♡ What did you want to be when you grew up?

Take a few minutes to look over your answers.

What still feels exciting to you?

2. **Go Ahead & Dream**
    ♡ What would be your top 5 dream jobs?

    ♡ In another life, I would….

    ♡ What would be your dream day off work?

    ♡ What would be your dream holiday?

    Which dream feels the most energizing and exciting right now?

3. **What do you admire?**
   Physical skills-

   Art forms-

   Sports-

   Music-

Careers-

Places-

What sparks you the most from these attributes?

4. Finish this sentence: if I had more time, I would…

    Is this possibly a passion?

5. Think about the people you have encountered in your life. What do they do that you admire?

    Are any of these things exciting to you?

6. If money wasn't an object, what would you be doing for fun?

7. What do you think you are horrible at, but do in privacy?

    Is this worth spending time on?

8. If you ever watch television, what type of shows are you drawn to?

    Is this something you want to do?

9. If you could go anywhere in the world, where would you go and why?

    Can you replicate what you are drawn to locally, or what do you need to do to make this dream trip happen?

10. Peruse the list of Creative things on page 29. Circle the ideas that seem interesting, or fun.

SCRIBE ALL OF YOUR POSSIBLE PASSIONS BASED ON THE Q&A ✏️

"Imagine there is a bank account that credits your account each morning with $86,400. It carries over no balance from day to day. Every evening the bank deletes whatever part of the balance you failed to use during the day.
What would you do? Draw out every cent, of course.

Each of us has such a bank, it's name is time.

Every morning, it credits you 86,400 seconds.
Every night it writes off at a loss, whatever of this you failed to invest to a good purpose. It carries over no balance.
It allows no over draft. Each day it opens a new account for you. Each night it burns the remains of the day.
If you fail to use the day's deposits, the loss is yours.
There is no drawing against "tomorrow".
You must live in the present on today's deposits.
Invest it so as to get from it the utmost in health, happiness, and health. The clock is running.
Make the most of today."

Marc Levy, "If Only it Were True"

Time seems to always be a factor. Regardless of career, or home life, we never seem to have enough time. Yet, truth be told, when we look closely at how we spend our time, we often find exactly the time that we need.

When it comes to finding time, it is about trade-offs, prioritizing and balancing.

On an average day…

1) How much time do you spend on social media? _____Minutes

2) How much time do you spend watching TV? _____Minutes

3) How much time do you spend on cooking, cleaning, and laundry? _____Minutes

4) How much time do you dedicate to the news, or current events? _____Minutes

♡ MULTIPLY the sum of these by 7

5) What are your work day obligations at home? _____Minutes

6) What else are you up to on a workday?
   Document the specifics:

   ♡ Guestimate your daily average _____Minutes. Multiply this
     sum by 5

7) How much spare time do you have on the weekend?
   ♡ _____Minutes

8) How much time per week would you like to spend pursuing
   your passion, or working on discovering it?
   _____Minutes

9) Make some tradeoffs! Where can you cut back, outsource, and
   make trades? It is up to you to find the time to pursue your
   passions!

10) Commit to it and prioritize this time.

the task: find the time to
PURSUE YOUR PASSIONS

	6-10 AM	10AM-12PM	12-2 PM	2-4 PM	4-6 PM	6-8 PM	8-10 PM
Monday							
Tuesday							
Wednesday							
Thursday							
Friday							
Saturday							
Sunday							

I AM COMMITTING TO SPEND:
_____ minutes per week
exploring my passions and
doing things that i love!

signed: _____

date: _____

63

LAUGHTER

IS PURE

HAPPINESS

AND

SOMETIMES IT

IS BEING SILLY

THAT HELPS

YOU GET THERE!

LET'S PLAY A GAME!
—— CHOOSE ——
A NUMBER BETWEEN 1
—— AND 50, ——
OR SCAN THE QR CODE
TO BE GIVEN
A RANDOM NUMBER

SCAN ME

MY NUMBER IS: _____

THE ART of Silly

In the shadows of my journey I can recall the essence of being a child: laughter, sport, jokes, play, creativity, belief, open-mindedness and of course silliness! The most fortunate children of this world approach the world with a strain of fun running through all that they do.

Somewhere along the journey many of us lose this because of the realities of our world: work, bills, relationships and most often because we do not give ourselves permission to do so. Yet, this very essence is re-ignited in the presence of children. Haven't you had an experience of being around a child and you find yourself acting and behaving in ways you never would with your adult friends?

Here is a question worth pondering: do you fully take advantage of all of the privileges of being an adult? Let's consider this for a moment…remember when you were young and all of those things that you weren't allowed to do seemed more fun? Well the truth is, now you CAN!!

This is **Great News** because when I really thought about it, I had a few things in my life I really wanted to do:

- jump on the bed
- eat ice cream in the bath
- have a pillow fight in the living room
- prank wars
- not make my bed
- eat chocolate for breakfast
- wear my Halloween costume to the grocery store
- stay up past "bed time" watching movies
- food fights

Maybe this list isn't all that appealing to you, but take a moment to think about whether, or not you take advantage of your privileges as an adult.

We may not be children anymore, but there is NOBODY to say that every once in a while we cannot connect with our inner child, chill out, have fun and act silly!

the self-love silly challenge:
use your number from page 65 and have fun
DOING THE CORRESPONDING ACTIVITY

1. Jump on your bed
2. Sing really loud
3. Dance wildly with total disregard for how you look
4. Eat something weird
5. Play a game of dare
6. Plan your day based on the wisdom of a magic 8 ball
7. Make and play with slime
8. Go out in silly PJs
9. Pledge a floor and slip around in your socks (warning this is slightly dangerous)
10. Randomly bust out the *running man* in public
11. Change the ringer on your phone to something funny
12. Improvise and make up a joke on the spot
13. Clean your house top to bottom (just joking)
14. Have a Jell-O, mud, water balloon, or food fight
15. Randomly sing Karaoke when you hear music in public
16. Host a Karaoke night
17. Choose what you will wear for the day blindfolded (maybe not a workday)
18. Watch kids movies and host a *slumber party*
19. Prank, or prank call someone with a good sense of humor
20. Spontaneously bust out exercise moves in public
21. Host a funny theme party and make it a contest - ugly sweater party anyone?

22. Finger paint, or body paint
23. The next time it rains, go play in puddles and the mud
24. Try singing in the rain
25. Dance in the rain
26. Practice juggling with eggs
27. Play tag
28. Play kick-the-can
29. Organize a capture the flag night in the dark
30. Ride your bicycle in a costume
31. Stay up late watching scary movies and make a spooky setting
32. Play "paint ball"
33. Make a DIY slip and slide
34. Go play at the park and swing on the swings
35. Randomly challenge someone to a swordfight with sticks
36. Play in the toy section at a department store
37. Go for a late night swim
38. Try a new sport: ice skating, roller blading, skiing etc.
39. Host a games night with your old favorites
40. Eat chocolate for breakfast
41. Do one thing you weren't allowed to when you were young
42. Run in the ocean with your clothes on
43. Have a video game night and invite friends/family to join
44. Start a random pillow fight
45. Do the *funky chicken* while waiting in line for groceries
46. Yell something at the top of your lungs
47. Jump rope & listen to your favorite music
48. Try a fun DIY science experiment (Mentos and diet coke?)
49. Have a bubble gum blowing contest
50. Learn how to do a magic trick, or cartwheel

LIFE
IS SO MUCH
BETTER WHEN
YOU TAKE
THE TIME
YOU NEED
TO CHILL OUT

THE CHILL OUT Q&A

1. What did you wish you had more time to do?

2. List 10 things that would feel like pampering right now:

3. Circle the answer that best suits your typical method of relaxation.
a) Watching T.V.
b) Looking online
c) Reading a book
d) Having a bath, or shower
e) Going for a walk

4. How many minutes per day do you get to relax?

5. Circle the answer that best matches your thoughts while relaxing?
a) Thank goodness. FINALLY!!!
b) I feel like I'm forgetting to do something?!
c) I really should be getting _____done.

♥ We ALL deserve to be pampered! Choose at least 2 items off your list (#2 of the Q & A) and enjoy the indulgence this week.

THE 7 DAY
CHILL OUT CHALLENGE

♥ Switch it up! Try 3 new paths to relaxation this week.

If you are stuck for ideas, choose from these:

- Meditation (page 92)
- Massage
- Listen to Relaxing Music
- Paint
- Yoga
- Go for a beach walk
- Hike and indulge in nature
- Enjoy a cup of tea
- Take time to be silent
- Garden
- Have a candlelit bubble bath
- Try any new mode of relaxation (whatever feels relaxing to you).
- **Try Coloring Page 72 &73**

♥ Pick it up a notch! Aim to double the amount of chill out time you have this week.

♥ <u>What was your answer to #5 in the Q&A?</u>

a) AWESOME!!! You really know how to kickback and chill. Keep doing what you are doing.

b) The Busy Brain Challenge: Spend 15 minutes per day this week emptying your mind. Listen to calming music and do not allow any thoughts enter into your mind. Be mindful of relaxing. This will be challenging at first, but after the 7 days it will get easier.

c) Letting go of the culture of BUSYNESS: Give yourself permission to relax with zero feelings of guilt. While relaxing, tell yourself, "It is natural to relax and I do not need to warrant my 'me' time." Each day work on giving yourself permission to just chill out.

WHEN

YOU LOVE YOURSELF,

RELAXATION IS NOT

a luxury.

IT IS A PRIORITY.

Forgiveness
        is a gift
            you give
            yourself.
            -Tony Robbins

Forgive with Gratitude

It is with gratitude that I forgive those who have wronged me because I am worth more than holding on to anger.

It is with gratitude that I forgive myself because I am worth more than holding onto guilt.

It is with gratitude that I forgive the universe for unfortunate circumstances because I am worth more than holding onto hate.

I can forgive because I love myself.

Many of us hold onto a plethora of negative emotions simply because we have yet to forgive. Sure, we have all made mistakes and some of them may continue to make a negative impact in our lives and the world around us. But here is the truth…guilt does nothing more than negatively impact our psyche and our health, so what is the point? For those of you who opt to feel guilty because you are punishing yourself, let's break that cycle today and begin the process of forgiveness. Forgiveness is imperative to self-love.

forgive yourself.

letting it out is the first step to letting go

TAKE ONE, OR MORE ITEMS FROM YOUR LIST AND ANSWER THE FOLLOWING:
 WHAT DID THIS EXPERIENCE TEACH YOU ABOUT YOURSELF?
WHAT DID THIS EXPERIENCE TEACH YOU ABOUT YOURSELF?
HOW ARE YOU GRATEFUL FOR THIS LEARNING EXPERIENCE?

i forgive because i love myself

The very best that we can do with regrets from our past is **learn.** Your life and your actions are inseparable from who you are. Some of your most profound learning experiences arise because of mistakes. You are not the same person you were when the mistake happened. You cannot change the past, but you can grow into the person you want to be.

Below what you have written, write down a quick sentence on how you are different from the person who made the mistake. *Who are you in this moment?*

And forgive that person, because you are no longer the same. You are wiser because of your experiences and it is pointless to hold onto negative emotions towards a prior version of yourself.

Forgiveness is to breathe the moment that is before you and to exhale what no longer serves you. It allows us to rise above our mistakes and gives us the freedom to be happy.

forgive others:

When we have forgiven ourselves, forgiving others suddenly becomes a lot easier. They too are not the same person who we continue to blame. They too have changed. We choose forgive others, not because they "deserve" it, but because we deserve freedom from the negativity. If we do not forgive others, the only person we are harming is ourselves.

Choose to forgive because YOU deserve freedom.

Write a Letter of Forgiveness:

Write a letter to who you are angry with. Keep in mind that you don't have to actually give it, just write it. In this letter, tell them exactly why you are angry:
- ♡ What have they done to wrong you?
- ♡ After you have done that, write down what this particular experience has taught you about yourself?
- ♡ What positive lessons has this challenging scenario given you?
- ♡ How can you be grateful?

Even our most challenging circumstances teach us something.
Next, write down "I forgive you." Take some time to read the letter and let it go. Choose to focus on the positive aspects (your learning experiences) and allow this message of growth permeate your truth.

Do what you want with the letter! Send it, burn it, rip it up etc.

The next time you begin to feel angry towards that person, in your mind return to the lesson that you learned. Be grateful for the teaching and move on.

a few mantras to tell yourself:

I forgive myself because I deserve a heart and mind full of love.

I only have room in my life for positive energy.

I love myself and who I have become.

I am growing into the best version of myself.

I do not judge myself. I do not judge others.

I forgive myself. I forgive others.

Today, I am a better person than who I was yesterday.

A house is
more than
a mere
shelter.
It should
lift
us
emotionally
&
spiritually.
-John Saladino

Create a Space for a
PEACEFUL MIND

Our physical environment can positively, or negative impact our psyche. Being between the walls of our home evokes an emotional response.

Ask Yourself & Record:

♡ How do I feel when I walk in the front door?

♡ How do I feel when I am in my living room, by bedroom, my kitchen?

If it not a positive response, think about what bothers you. Strive to create a place that reflects your *emotional intentions.*

Tips for Recreating your Space:

♡ Choose a desired *feeling* for each room. In your kitchen, you may want to feel inspired, or energized. In your bedroom, you may want to feel romantic, or calm.

Record how do you want your space to feel?

Kitchen:

Dining Space:

Restroom:

Living Space:

Bedroom:

Wardrobe:

Office (if applicable):

Outdoor Space (if any):

Check off what spaces already accomplish your emotional desire.

♡ Choose one space at a time. Changes don't have to be expensive, or cost any money at all. Either way, you are choosing to invest time in making a positive change for your emotional well-being.

♡ Start with decluttering and organizing. Donate, sell, and keep in mind that less is often more! Don't focus on the perceived financial loss, focus on the emotional gain.

♡ Consider electronic free zones, or times. For instance, you may decide that you want your dining space to feel energizing. Do the use of electronics help, or hinder that? Experiment with the idea and play around with what works for you and your household!

♡ Add one thing that will make a big change. For instance, I made the decision to add fresh flowers to my outdoor writing space each week. I don't purchase them, I take the time to pick wildflowers. They give me energy, inspire and infuse me with more creativity. The choice is really personal. For you, it may be painting the walls, some type of organizational unit, a new teapot, etc.

♡ Be creative and have fun. Your changes do not need to be conventional. Get inspired by thinking outside of the box.

♡ Incorporate plants. When we bring our natural world into the home, it is not only relaxing, the extra oxygen is good for your health too.

♡ Get others involved!

If music
— B E —
THE FOOD
of LOVE,
play on.
— William Shakespeare —

SELF-LOVE AND YOUR RELATIONSHIP WITH FOOD

Our relationship with food is intricately connected with our state of self-love. Whether it is a love story, an inspirational narrative, or a tragedy, everyone has a food story: too much, not enough, I love it, it is my nemesis, it is my passion, I only eat healthy, or I can't afford to eat healthy. Most of our stories evolve with us and our relationship with food shifts as we do.

Honor your food story with our

INSPIRATIONAL WRITING CHALLENGE

Write your food story beginning with childhood. Detail how your relationship with food has evolved over the years. End the story with an inspirational ending (this is where you include your goals). This creative writing will honor your personal evolution, self-love, and give you a space to visualize your future. Be true to your emotions, goals, beliefs, challenges and triumphs!

Challenge yourself
TO DISCONNECT TO RECONNECT!
GO 24 HOURS WITHOUT TV, COMPUTERS, VIDEO GAMES, CELL PHONES, OR TABLETS.
STARTING...NOW

~~~~~~~~

THE PRESENT MOMENT
IS FILLED WITH JOY
and happiness.
IF YOU ARE ATTENTIVE,
YOU WILL SEE IT.
—thich nhat hanh

PRACTICING MINDFULNESS:
The Art of Presence

Although mindfulness is a practice that derived from Buddhist tradition, it has evolved over the years to become common practice for yogis, self-help gurus, psychologists and of course the everyday being.

Being mindful has a slew of benefits that will hopefully entice you into this practice: decreases stress, lowers anxiety, reduces feelings of loneliness, gives you the opportunity to know yourself better, promotes empathy, increases compassion, helps sleep, lowers the risk of depression, helps you be more aware/intuitive, improves memory, better focus and overall improved life satisfaction.

So What Is Mindfulness?

In the simplest terms, to be mindful is to be fully present without judgement. It is intentionally being fully aware of your thoughts, sensations, and feelings as they occur in the moment.

14 MINDFUL PRACTICES
The Two Week Challenge

Note: The length of time is up to you! **Try small intervals at first. Be aware of your emotional and breathing shifts.**

Day 1: Be alone in nature and simply observe. Listen to the sounds as they happen. What does the air feel and smell like? What is happening with your energy?

Day 2: In the shower, try making a mental note of all of the sensations. How does the water feel? Tune into your body. Listen to the sounds.

Day 3: During conversations be intent on staying in the moment. Do not allow your mind slip to past experiences/memories. Pay attention to your energy.

Day 4: Be mindful while eating. Focus on the flavor, the feeling of the food on your tongue, texture, sound and smell.

Day 5: Be aware of your emotions while you listen to music. How do you feel while each song feels? Do you have any physical reactions? Listen to each word as it is sung. Focus on the instruments. Try this with your favorite songs. You may be surprised what you hear.

Day 6: Go for a walk and for 60 seconds focused on the feelings of each step. Pay attention to your feet, to your breath, and your energy.

Day 7: Throughout the day, pause and take note of your senses: touch, taste, smell, sight and sound.

Day 8: Try taking some time to be alone in silence. What is going on around you and within you?

Day 9: Use being present in times of stress. Often we worry about things that are beyond our control, or are not related to the moment. Focus your feelings and thoughts on the moment.

Day 10: Try being mindful while doing something creative.

Day 11: When a negative thought enters into your mind, go somewhere quiet and replace it with a positive thought. Be aware of your emotional shift.

Day 12: While sitting or waiting, focus on your posture and breath.

Day 13: Star gaze and only pay attention to your senses.

Day 14: Be fully present in a situation where you would normally feel irritated, or rushed (line ups, commute to work etc.)

Get Techy: Check out mindful meditations on YouTube.
    Try a mindfulness app – there is a ton out there!

In her sweet
innocence,
she captured
what I had
struggled
with for much
of my adult life...
-Dani Nir-McGrath

Breathe.
REMEMBER YOU ARE LOVED

Dani Nir-McGrath
Co-Creator of Spiritual Junkies &
Manifesting Mamas

I am a recovering people-pleaser. For years, I couldn't
use the word "no" and piled on more and more and more in the hopes of helping others.
Then, the greatest lesson in self-love was gifted to me unintentionally by my youngest
child, who's now 5 years old. This beautiful, insightful and inquisitive child's thoughts,
actions and words are well beyond her years.

I found her in my bathroom going through my toiletries after dressing up in her favorite
dress and jewels. First she covered her little arms and legs with lotion. Then she
lovingly sprayed conditioner in her long blond hair and brushed out her curls. Then she
selected her favorite lip gloss of mine and placed it on her plump little lips. Once she
was complete, she looked in the mirror and said "What else, mommy? What else can I
do for myself?"

Her words have echoed in me because in her sweet innocence, she captured what I'd
struggled with for much of my adult life. The act of self-love and self-care is absolutely
second nature to her.

As a single mother, I had so many deeply ingrained beliefs about putting others, namely
my children, first in order to be a good mom. But 4 years ago, at the time of my
separation and subsequent divorce, I struggled with doing anything for myself. My
actions and world revolved around two young children and I found myself neglected,
and ultimately unhealthy and worn out.

Her lesson was timely and its effects have rippled into other areas of my life. Here are a
few of those ways:

- ♡ We must first care for ourselves in order to be of any good to others. An
  empty vessel simply has nothing to pour into another!

- ♡ Nurturing ourselves, body, mind and spirit, is necessary to live a balanced life.
- ♡ Giving to ourselves does not deplete others. We live in an abundant world, and there is enough for us all.
- ♡ How we treat ourselves is a reflection of how others will ultimately treat us.
- ♡ Loving ourselves leads to many more loving relationships in our lives.
- ♡ Being a shining example of loving and giving to ourselves, allows others to do the same.

Show Yourself Love:

- ♡ Prepare your favorite meal, even if you're dining alone!
- ♡ Stop saving your finest dishware, bottle of wine or candles for future guests…indulge yourself!
- ♡ Do the little things: light candles, burn incense or use essential oils, take a bubble bath, and listen to music that makes you feel good
- ♡ Get active! Talk a walk, go to an exercise class, or practice a few yoga poses.
- ♡ Be outside and enjoy Mother Nature.
- ♡ Surround yourself with things and people that bring a smile to your face.
- ♡ Feed your soul. Read. Remind yourself of what you're grateful for NOW. Meditate. Pray. Paint. Sing. Dance. Or whatever makes your heart happy!
- ♡ BREATHE. Remember you are loved.

Aside from the ongoing lessons of motherhood, my second greatest lesson in self-love has been through yoga and meditation. And in the process of re-discovering yoga over the past few years and becoming a certified yoga instructor, I found so clearly that self-love, acceptance, non judgement, surrender…it was a way of being. It could not be mastered once, but instead it is a constant practice that led me to love and to accept all of me on a deeper level.

Centering Self-Love Excercise

Sit with your legs crossed on a mat or blanket. Allow your fingertips to lightly touch the floor by your side body. Feel yourself getting grounded and connected to the earth below you. Imagine a string at the crown of your head lifting and lengthening your spine. Gently tuck in your chin and release your shoulders down away from your ears.

Take a moment to tap into your breath. Place one hand on your heart and your other hand on your belly. Notice the belly and chest rising and falling. And as you do, begin to slow the breath. Imagine every inhale as love entering your body. As you do this, perhaps giving the love a texture or color. Trace its path through your body as you fill with love. As you exhale, imagine love being sent out into the world.

After becoming comfortable with this breath, begin to cultivate a mantra for each breath. Silently repeat, "I inhale love" followed by, "I exhale love." Stay here as long as you choose.

When you're ready, release your hands to the side of your body. Wiggle the fingers bringing movement to the body and allow them to brush the mat or floor at your side body. On the inhale, raise your arms out and up bringing them overhead until the palms touch. Exhale and release the hands to the heart. Press the thumbs gently into your chest. Allow the hands at your heart as a reminder to feel love and kindness towards yourself. Raise the hands to the lips as a reminder to speak words of love and kindness towards yourself. And lastly, raise your hands to your third eye as a reminder to think thoughts of love and kindness towards yourself. Inhale one last time; and exhale, letting it go.

SCAN ME
for the guided audio

Namaste

AS YOU BREATHE IN, CHERISH YOURSELF.
AS YOU BREATHE OUT, CHERISH ALL BEINGS
THE 14TH DALAI LAMA

GIVE LOVE:

CAUSE SOMEONE TO

EXPERIENCE

LOVE

The Hole in
THE WALL

One of the extraordinary gifts of travel is that it allows us to learn ways of living that often contrast our norms. Often, we have said, "Just remember, it is the opposite." You can take the strange and bizarre for what it is, and embrace the pieces you love. Foreign cultures not only give us a heightened sense of gratitude to our homelands, they also show us new ways of being a better version of self. Wherever we go, we are able to adapt and adopt the customs and thoughts we connect with and they become integral threads in the fabric of who we are. That is the beauty of learning on the road. Regardless of how small of a bag you fit your life in, this is the stuff you really need to carry with you.

I remember having a long conversation with a Canadian friend who was on a journey of rediscovering and reconnecting with self. He was taking a short pause from his chaos to re-evaluate and reconstruct his way of living. Beyond the laughs and light hearted jokes, the heart of the conversation was kindness. We explained to him how overwhelmed we were with the kindness of our neighbors.

We told him about the time we were living in a little Thai village where we were the only foreigners. The long and uncomfortable stares from the locals were our daily reminder of just how little we fit in. In the back of the small home we were renting was a semi-outdoor laundry room. When we first moved in, we observed the oddity that the wall did not meet the ceiling. The two foot gap at the top of the wall was shared between the back of our home and the home of the house behind us. We couldn't see anything, but we certainly could hear everything. We could hear the voices clearly chattering, the occasional full throttle singing through the hole and all we could think of is how this *unfinished* wall infringed on our privacy. We felt vulnerable to this space. But, over the course of the eight months that we resided there, we came to realize just how powerful an opening in a wall can be.

One night while we fumbled around in the kitchen in the stifling forty degree heat, we could hear our neighbors doing the same. Over the wall, the overwhelming, suffocating waft of chilies had drifted into our home. As amateurs to the intensity, we both coughed. We could hear the neighbor's laughter and we thought, surely they had heard us. Then a quiet and insistent voice spoke, "neighbor? Neighbor?" We glanced at each other uncomfortably, knowing she was speaking to us and responded affirmatively. This little voice wanted to enquire whether we had dinner. We told her we hadn't. Through the gap in the wall, she reached her hand over the wall and held out a small plastic bag of curry. We thanked her for her generosity and ate the food that she provided. That was the first of many occasions that would follow. Through the hole in the wall our neighbor became our friend. From offering assistance of light in power outages, small gifts, to personal conversations about the direction of my relationship with Rob. Although we never saw each other, or met beyond that wall, we were friends.

In the same way I have now explained these acts of kindness, we detailed our experiences to our Canadian friend. He explained how he wished his apartment building had that sense of community and kindness. He wished their relationships were more than the obligatory greetings in the hallway.

The lesson was clear. Be kind first.

Go out of your way to ACT in the way that you want to be treated. If you want kind neighbors, DO something kind for them. It is truly up to all of us to ALL of us to create more love in the world.

So, Gandhi's wisdom was right…

WHAT CHANGES DO YOU WANT TO SEE IN THE WORLD?

ALL BIG CHANGES, START WITH INDIVIDUAL ACTION.

Here are a few ideas to get you started:

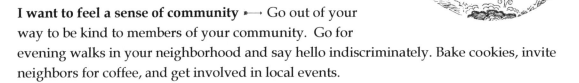

I want to feel a sense of community •—→ Go out of your way to be kind to members of your community. Go for evening walks in your neighborhood and say hello indiscriminately. Bake cookies, invite neighbors for coffee, and get involved in local events.

I want to see people treat the environment better •—→Take initiative, be proactive and invite your friends to join you. Look at your body and your consumption as a microcosm of the bigger picture. Hate pesticides? Eat organic. Tired of local stores closing to foreign business? Shop locally and don't buy from the businesses you don't agree with. Try going for a rubbish collection beach walk, or hike through the forest. Start an awareness campaign, or join an existing one that you connect with.

I wish people weren't so grumpy •—→ Be nice to EVERYONE and that includes all of the grumpy ones. Start by smiling at all of the strangers you pass by in a day. Better yet, start saying hello too. Yes, your cheeks will be sore, but your happiness will be contagious to others.

I wish that everyone had food to eat •—→ Start with yourself. What can you do in your household to save money, so that you can give more back? How can you reduce food waste? Cook your favorite meal and deliver it to someone, or many people in need. Start a veggie garden and donate the excess food.

I wish there was less suffering •—→ What can you do to reduce the suffering locally, or internationally? Can you donate food, money, or time? Lonliness is suffering too. Be a friend to someone who needs a listening ear? Start a free drop in course and offer your expertise to people who cannot afford education.

I wish people treated animals humanely ⬦—→ Reevaluate your lifestyle. Is there anything that you do that contributes to the suffering of animals? What can you personally do to change? Donate time, money or energy promoting the cause you feel passionate about. Keep in mind that your concerns will differ from the opinions of others and that is okay.

I wish people would stop criticizing others ⬦—→ Watch your thoughts and what you say for one day. Are you a part of the problem? Ask loved ones, friends and family if you are being critical. Be open and receptive to their thoughts. Make it your personal goal to stop all forms of criticism to yourself and others. Respect and be grateful for diversity, even when you don't agree.

It drives me crazy when all people do is gossip ⬦—→ Who have you said that to, and about who? That in itself is gossiping. Yes, it can be a tough one for some to give up. Watch your thoughts and monitor your conversation (on social media too!). Give it up.

I can't stand fake people ⬦—→ Start with being more genuine. How many different personas do you have in your life? It is a lifelong journey for many, but we all truly aim to be "one being". Remember the judgment you get from others is a reflection of them. In the same breath, we need to strive for non-judgement of others. We should all aim for embracing diversity, rather than tolerating it.

I wish people would accept themselves ⬦—→ Repeatedly, people tell us that they are learning to "accept" themselves. Let's aim higher. Let's love and embrace ourselves and our uniqueness (not flaws). Since we have all come to agree that all beings are imperfect, it only seems fair to stop looking at these differences as "flaws". The word in itself suggests there is something other than flawed which we all know does not exist. Change your language to reflect the truth. Love yourself first.

I want world peace ⬦—→ Begin by resolving ANY and ALL conflict in your life and work outward. Start within. Do you hate anyone? Begin the process of forgiveness. Do you think negative thoughts about yourself? Be conscious and think kind thoughts (yes, compliment yourself too)! Do you argue with people? Stop! It does take two people and if you aren't one of them, they don't happen. After you have peace with yourself, and your circles, move outward. What can you do to make your neighborhood, city, state, country, and world more peaceful?

By no means is this list exhaustive, nor is it meant to be (that would be a whole book in itself). This is a starting place for you to give more love. Start small and it will avalanche. Positive change has an extraordinary ripple effect.

CREATE YOUR "BE THE CHANGE" ACTION PLAN

make these fortune cookies with love

AND GIVE THEM AWAY

RECIPE:

3 tablespoons of butter (reserve 1/2 tablespoon to grease the pan)

2 egg whites

½ cup sugar

½ cup flour

1 ½ tablespoon of cream

Pinch of Salt

½ teaspoon of vanilla or almond extract

INSTRUCTIONS:

1) Have your inspirational messages cut and ready to go. There are premade ones included on page 105.

2) Watch the video on how to fold the baked fortune cookie. Scan the code below and skip to 2 minutes and 30 seconds. Cut out the circle guide on page 107 and get your glasses for moulding the cookies ready.
3) Preheat oven to 400° F (205° C).
4) Use the ½ tablespoon of reserved butter to lightly grease the pan. You will need to do this each time you bake.
5) Melt the remaining butter on the stovetop, or in the microwave.
6) Using an electric mixer, or a whisk, combine the egg whites and sugar. Beat for 30 seconds on medium with the electric mixer, or 2 minutes briskly with your whisk.
7) Stir in your melted butter, salt and extract.
8) Now for the fun part! Scoop one tablespoon of batter on the baking pan and spread with the back of the spoon to make a 5 inch circle. Use the guide to help you with your measurement. Bake one at a time until you get the hang of it.
9) Bake for approximately 8 minutes, or until the edges are golden brown.
10) Get ready to work quickly. While the cookie is hot, it is pliable. Once it is cooled too much, it hardens. Lift the cookie off the pan and use a wooden cutting board, or kitchen towel to rest the spatula while you work. Place the fortune in the center. Fold the cookie in half (into a semi-cirle) and bend the cookie in the center to drape over a glass/coffee mug to cool.
11) Repeat the baking and creating process until your batter is finished.
12) Voila! Baking with love complete. Give them away with love and make someone's day extra special!

Cut out these inspirational fortunes and place them inside of your cookies!

You are so talented. Share it!	You are beautiful, wise and loved!
Keep your head held high :)	Your smile and laughter ROCKS!
Follow your dreams and believe!	You are appreciated beyond words
You deserve pure happiness!	You deserve to be pampered! Do it
Your intuition is wise. Listen more	Celebrate your AWESOMENESS
You are beautiful exactly as you are	Your strength is INSPIRING!!!

105

Cut Me Out &
Use me as your
Guide

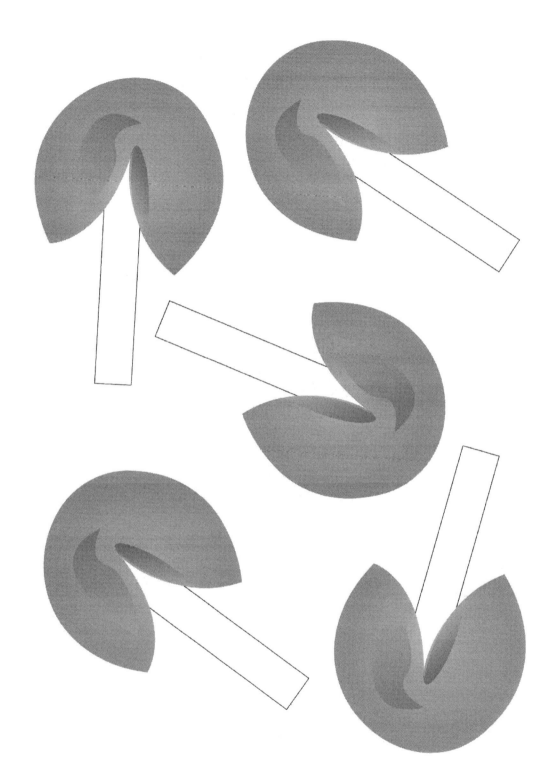

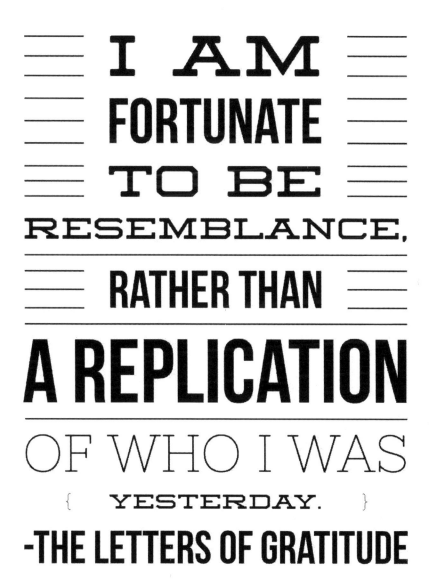

I AM
FORTUNATE
TO BE
RESEMBLANCE,
RATHER THAN
A REPLICATION
OF WHO I WAS
{ YESTERDAY. }

-THE LETTERS OF GRATITUDE

LOVE & RESPECT THE EVOLUTION OF OTHERS

Our memories are often like nostalgic photographs. We take a mental snapshot of the people in our lives at a particular moment in time. This is how we choose to know them. Whether the moment is a positive, or a negative, we tend to capture people and *lock them in* as this particular person. When they act in ways that differ from this particular image, we call them on it, or we judge them on our idea of who they are. We say or think things like "they aren't themselves today", or "they are acting strange." Worse yet, we view them as *fake*, or *liars* because they are no longer *who we thought they were*. This leads to the breakdown of all types of relationships: friendships are lost, marriages are ended, and families are split apart.

Take a few moments to look back 5 years, 10 years, or 20 years in your life. Regardless of the nomination chose, ask yourself:

- ♡ Who were you?
- ♡ What were you doing?
- ♡ What did you believe in?
- ♡ Who did you love?
- ♡ What did you love?
- ♡ What did you love about them?
- ♡ What did you eat?
- ♡ What were you passionate about?
- ♡ What did you want for your future?

Take a few moments to mentally create that picture in your mind. Now ask yourself the same questions about yourself in this moment. It is often surprising how much we evolve in our lives, how much we change, and how much we no longer resemble our former selves. Knowing this, it seems unfair and ridiculous to think anyone else is different.

Growth is imperative and should therefore be free of our emotional judgment.

Being aware of this, we can do our very best to honor, love, encourage, and respect the evolution of others.

CHECK YOURSELF:

Choose a person you are close with. The people you have the longest relationships with work the best for your reflection.

Name: _____

1. **Write in detail how you view them and what you love about them.**

   Spend an hour with this person and come back to answer the next question.

2. **Imagine that one hour you spent with that person is the only time you knew them. Write in detail how you view them and what you love about them.**

3. **Compare the two. What is new? What is entirely different? What is the same?**

While an hour with a person doesn't capture their entire essence or being, it does give us an idea of whether, or not we acknowledge and value the growth of the people we care about. Getting to know who they are now, is just as important as our memories of them.

HOW TO LOVE & RESPECT THEIR EVOLUTION

♡ Check in regularly and ask people what they are loving right now, instead of asking what is new.

♡ Honor the authenticity of who you surround yourself by not measuring them up against who you know.

♡ Give people space to make their own decisions. Avoid persuading people to following what you believe to be right. Listening is caring. Advising is selfish. Instead, ask questions that help people find their truth.

♡ Avoid critical language such as, "you are just not the person I know!" "Why can't you be yourself?" Of course they have changed! YAHOO

♡ Cheer people on when you notice positive changes. "Hey, I noticed you have been really into running lately. That's awesome!"

♡ Think of the types of questions you ask people when you first meet them. Ask them again. This will help to get to know who the person is now. Just because someone answered something one way, does not permanently lock them in that perspective, or opinion.

♡ Try to think of spending time with people as getting to know them. Regardless of how well you think you know someone, adapt your image of who they were with who they are!

♡ Be free of judgment when observing others. Do your best not to measure people up to *your* vision of who they are. Be open to who they are with the understanding it may change your relationship. In friendships, or relationships this can come as a shock and sometimes growth can distances people, or sever the relationship. You can respect their growth and realize that the relationship is no longer beneficial.

NEVER APOLOGIZE FOR WHAT YOU FEEL. IT'S LIKE SAYING SORRY FOR BEING REAL.

— Unknown —

7 THINGS WE APOLOGIZE FOR EVERYDAY,

but Shouldn't

Apologetic language floods our day to day conversations so much so that it is beginning to lose meaning, value, and sincerity. We say "sorry" so often that we are probably unaware of exactly how often we use it. Saying sorry when we don't mean it can be a dangerous miscommunication hiding what we are really trying to express.

Acknowledge it and strive to communicate with authenticity.

7 Things we Apologize for:

1) **Our Personal Appearance.** *Sorry my hair is messy. I wasn't expecting to see anyone.* Does our appearance really warrant an apology? Is it offending anyone? Likely, it isn't. When we apologize for appearance we are essentially saying that the way we look isn't *good enough* for the company. Regardless of how you appear, love yourself as you are and don't apologize for it.

2) **Our bodily functions**. *Sorry I am sweaty, but I just went for a run.* Really? When we apologize for sweat, we are suggestion that our body functioning correctly is negative. It doesn't seem like this is something we should be sorry about. Rather, we should be celebrating our good health.

3) **Disagreeing in conversation**. *I am sorry, but I disagree.* Apologizing for a different opinion suggests that having your own thoughts has a negative connotation. Since when did diversity become a bad thing? Perhaps, we could just respectfully disagree and enjoy the good conversation.

4) **Other People's Emotions**. *I am sorry you're mad.* Apologizing for other people's emotions suggests that we have some level of control over them. Wouldn't that be cool if we did? Maybe, not. People are in charge and have control on their own individual responses. For instance, let's say you chose to not do the dishes and your spouse comes home to a sink full

of dishes. You see their anger and then apologize. They could react in a variety of ways: laugh, ignore them, or do the dishes with no reaction at all. The point is that despite what you did, every individual is responsible for their emotions, not you. The same can be said for positive emotions too.

5) **Other People's Behaviors**. *I am sorry that my Dad is so blunt.* You have zero control over the behaviors around you, except your own. Apologizing on someone's behalf suggests that you have done something wrong. We can feel embarrassed, sad, or even angry for other's behavior, but their behaviors are not ours to apologize for. Their actions are a reflection of them, not you.

6) **Our emotional state**. *I am sorry that I am talking so fast. It's just that I am really excited.* Or, *I am sorry I am not happy. I am having a bad day.* Own them, own them, own them. I will say it again, own your emotions! If you want to change how you feel, than do it. If not, don't excuse them, embrace them.

7) **Our Oddities**. *I am sorry that I am so weird.* So you are a bit "out there", or "totally out there", that's great! Don't apologize for being yourself because you would feel really sorry if you weren't.

We often apologize for things that we have zero control over, or about things that don't warrant an apology whatsoever. We use it to self-criticize, to excuse who we are, and how we are feeling. We should strive to embrace our eclecticism, and celebrate our individuality, not apologize for it. When we express regret for things that we aren't really sorry about, our apologies lose sincerity. Think about that for a minute. How much is someone's apology worth when only 10 minutes prior they apologized about the messiness of their hair? If you are finding that people don't respond to your apologies, try to save saying sorry for when it really counts. Be authentic with who you are and stop apologizing for it.

TOO MUCH DRAMA ON SOCIAL MEDIA? *Let this be* A REMINDER OF WHO YOU SURROUND YOURSELF WITH.

GIVE LOVE ♥ ON SOCIAL MEDIA

After writing *The Letters of Gratitude* we would scroll through our Facebook feed and become overwhelmed with the amount of online negativity. These were the lives of our friends, family members and our colleagues. This is who we surrounded ourselves with.

OUR LESSONS FROM SOCIAL MEDIA

- We took the time to reevaluate our friendships. Although it sounds drastic, it was and still is, imperative to our well-being and happiness. In some cases, our shift to focusing on positivity was not reflected, or respected by our circles. We choose to surround ourselves with positive people.
- We understand that we all rant sometimes. Sometimes it is about sharing experience, lessons and in the end this helps the greater good of people. People review honestly and that is commendable.
- We realized there was a need for an online space of positivity. Keep in mind, this is going back four years. So we did what we could to become a part of positive change on our social networks.
- We appreciated that we were a part of the problem. We were participating and then complaining about the negativity to each other. The hypocrisy makes no sense, but applying concepts in our own world takes time. After this awareness, we evolved. We stopped joining negative conversations online, we stopped giving them a thumbs up, we stopped participating in what we viewed as a problem.

GIVE LOVE ♥ ON SOCIAL MEDIA

♡   Start with yourself. Do you post updates simply to vent or put other people down? Do you use social media to complain? Share the good news. That is not to say that challenges don't exist, but there is always something positive to take away from these experiences, be sure to share that too!

♡　Stop joining in on negative conversations that go nowhere. There are times when reviewing, or commenting create compelling conversations and that is okay. But if the intention/outcome is not positive, than what is the point? When you see negative conversations either move on, or comment with a positive spin.

♡　Like, comment and share positive posts. Sometimes, we have the tendency to scroll by these posts, but take the time to offer a congratulations, or kudos. Spread and share good news, informative articles, and positive movements/campaigns.

♡　Be social. Make meaningful connections and go out of your way to keep in touch with people you care about.

♡　After posting, stop using the feedback (likes/retweets/views) you're given as a measure of love. Find the balance between accepting the love you are given with loving yourself first.

♡　Be genuine. Share the unflattering photos and forget about the editing, or filtering every photo. That is the truth. A lot of people tell us, they wish their circles were more genuine. Well, start with yourself! Is your social media a true reflection of you, or an extremely edited version? Some people will say they don't want everyone knowing everything. In that case, perhaps it is time to slim down your circles. Be vulnerable and be yourself.

♡　Don't take it too seriously. Have fun.

♡　Be empathetic and supportive. See someone having a tough time? Offer a listening ear, offer your empathy, and be compassionate.

Join in on the positive online conversations by using #thebookoflove We will do our best to respond to all of your thoughts!

Connect with loving people and groups! Check out page 217 for suggestions

ALL POSITIVE ACTIONS, GRAND OR SMALL, MAKE THE WORLD A MORE LOVING PLACE.

• SUGAR SCRUB MADE WITH LOVE •

Everyone deserves to be pampered, but not all of us get many opportunities to do so. Choose to make this gift for the men, or women in your life who could use a little extra sweetness in their world. Everybody is different, so take the time to choose your unique additions based on the persons individuals tastes. This thoughtful act and personalized gift is a super sweet and loving gesture!

Base Recipe:

½ cup Extra Virgin Coconut Oil, Olive Oil, or Almond Oil (adjust the amount of oil based on your preferred consistency).

1 cup of Sugar (brown, or white)

½ teaspoon of vitamin E oil (optional)

Choose your additions. Be creative and have fun!

EXTRACTS:

Extracts can be found in the baking isle of your supermarket

- ♡ Peppermint Extract
- ♡ Almond Extract
- ♡ Vanilla Extract
- ♡ Lemon Extract
- ♡ Raspberry Extract

Appearance Enhancers:

- ♡ Sparkles (available at craft shops)
- ♡ Food Coloring

From the Pantry:

- ♡ Cinnamon Powder
- ♡ Pumpkin Pie Spice
- ♡ Coffee Grounds
- ♡ Cocoa Powder
- ♡ Shaved white, dark, milk chocolate
- ♡ Honey
- ♡ Dried Rosemary
- ♡ Crushed hard Candies (peppermint, butterscotch, valentine's heart candies with messages, kopiko etc.)
- ♡ Coconut Flakes (you can color them too if you like)

- ♡ Toasted Coconut Flakes
- ♡ Oatmeal
- ♡ Jasmine Tea, Chai Tea, or Green Tea
- ♡ 4-5 Herbal Tea Bags of your Choice Flavor (sleepy, chamomile, peach, raspberry etc.) Open the pouches and pour them in.
- ♡ Matcha Green Tea Powder

Fresh Additions:

When using some fresh fruit, or herbs the scrub will not last as long. You may wish to refrigerate to store.

- ♡ Peeled &Pureed Aloe Vera
- ♡ Ginger
- ♡ Dried, or Fresh Flowers Petals (lavender, roses)
- ♡ Pureed Fruit, or berries (apple, cranberries, grapefruit, oranges, pineapple, raspberries, bananas, blueberries, blackberries)
- ♡ Pureed Cucumber
- ♡ Fresh Mint
- ♡ Rosemary
- ♡ Orange, Lemon, or Lime Zest & Juice

NOTE: you can also use essential oils if you have the cash (they tend to be expensive). If you do go this way, be sure to carefully research the safety precautions.

make 2 sugar scrubs for gifts to loved ones.

USE THE INSTRUCTIONS

TO HELP GUIDE THE CREATION OF YOUR SPECIAL BLENDS!

CUT OUT THE PRE-MADE LABELS BELOW AND ADHERE TO THE JAR OF YOUR CHOICE.

Sugar Scrub
Made with LOVE
To:
From:

Sugar Scrub
Made with LOVE
To:
From:

RECORD YOUR RECIPES

THERE

is an amazing sense

OF COMMUNITY

and togetherness that

a garden can gather.

A GARDEN invitation

We had the great fortune of renting a friend's house for a month during the summer of 2014. One of the joyous perks was her garden. For anyone who has had the experience of fresh picked fruit and vegetables, you too know that nothing can compare to that pureness. Eating food directly from the ground, or off the tree takes me home, to childhood memories and reminds me just how privileged we are. During that summer, we began to have a hard time eating to the pace of the growth, but we soon came to realize that haste would soon come to an ease.

I suppose one of the downsides of not being in a particular place for long, is you lose some of the simplest and most beautiful processes of nurturing a garden. You are never quite somewhere long enough to watch the seeds grow into their maturity. There is something inexplicably magical about being a part of the growth and well-being of something beyond yourself. That summer I did have the privilege of seeing the amazing sense of community and togetherness that a garden can gather.

Our friend's garden was not only hers, she had invited friends and loved ones to come and go as they pleased. They could come and pick what they needed and move on. She was not only able to feed her family, but also contribute to happiness of her community.

If you do have space to grow food, consider taking the time to start a garden. Create an environment where you can invite neighbors to "help themselves". Have a "free veggie" stand with any excess. Donate this nutritious food to a local shelter. Consider sharing your land and love with those in your community.

Random Acts of LOVE

We can all agree that the world could be kinder, more loving and selfless. The best way to see this shift happen is to give our love indiscriminately and often! You have the power to change someone's day, or life for the better. The results of our acts are usually unknown and we never fully know the true impact that they have on someone's life. But, every once in a while the true impact of your acts will reveal themselves to you and sometimes it will leave you in awe! This is your confirmation, if you need any, that your path of love is a rewarding way of life.

Close to a year ago, we felt the intent urge to write a letter to our followers. Time and again, we would receive messages crying for help, looking for advice, seeking some sort of online approval because they were not getting the support they needed in their life. And so we wrote a letter to everyone (on page 156). It took us a few hours, but we were happy to use this time to express ourselves to those in needed to hear those words. It simply felt like the right thing to do. We posted in on our website, social groups, and let it go. It wasn't long before we received a heartfelt email:

I was going to kill myself, but after reading this I have changed my mind. Thank you.

Those few hours of our time, energy and love were certainly of value. They equated to a human life. This is of course an extreme, but the old cliché rings true: we can make the world a better place one act at a time. Slow down, look around, and listen the beckons of your heart.

Random Acts of Love
Cut this page. Toss a Coin. Give LOVE. Use Often

Give 10 Smiles to Strangers

Leave an inspirational book in a public place

Write and give 3 Thank You Cards.

Bake a dessert and give it to a neighbor.

Feed a stranger a nutritious meal on you!

Hug 5 People that you never have

Plant something beautiful in public.

Buy your favorite drink and give it away.

Offer 1 hour of your time to help someone.

Teach someone one of your talents.

Give out 5 Compliments to strangers.

Clean your closet and donate.

Give out 5 treats to strangers.

Make a stranger laugh.

Pick up someone's tab based on an amount you choose to give

Cut this Page. Write Loving Notes & Post them for people you love, or in public places for strangers!

100 ACTS OF LOVE:
Use this list often

1. Tip ridiculously (especially if someone seems to be having a challenging day).
2. Feed someone.
3. Host a Free Hugs Day.
4. Buy flowers and attach a loving note. Give them away to strangers.
5. Deliver anonymous love letters to mailboxes.
6. Compliment strangers.
7. Bake something and randomly give it away.
8. Put loving notes in balloons. Write "pop me" on the outside and give them away.
9. Put a kind message in a bottle and send it off.
10. Start a conversation with someone who seems to be struggling.
11. Invest in micro-loans (check out Kiva.org)
12. Give kind notes/thank you cards for people in the service industry that you appreciate, but have yet to extend thanks (gas stations, grocery stores, coffee shops etc.).
13. Give gift certificates to your favorite places to strangers.
14. Gift wrap something special with a meaningful note and give it to someone in need.
15. Pick up a strangers bill and tell them to pass on the love.
16. Start a give back business.
17. Be mindful while shopping. Support businesses that give to a good cause! Check out GiveGeneration.com
18. Pick something from the creativity list and give it away.

19. Adopt a pet from a local shelter, or donate your time.
20. Leave your favorite inspirational book in a public place.
21. Do something kind for the environment. Spend a day picking up litter etc.
22. Spend time with people who are lonely.
23. Leave an uplifting note taped to the mirror in a public restroom.
24. Declutter and Donate.
25. Spend one day focused on smiling at everyone you see.
26. Spend one day focused solely on listening to people.
27. Call people and thank them for specific things you appreciate.
28. Communicate with a local shelter and ask them what type of support they need. Act.
29. Go out of your way to introduce yourself to neighbors.
30. Give your time to community events.
31. What are you awesome at? Offer to teach someone free of charge!
32. Call a local school, or program and ask what they need? Is there something you could do to support them?
33. Invent something that will help people.
34. Start a veggie garden and donate the food.
35. On occasions where you would normally receive gifts, donate them instead of keeping them.
36. Have a garage sale and donate the proceeds.
37. Foster an animal until it can find a permanent home.
38. Cook your favorite meal and deliver it to someone in need.
39. Buy tickets to a movie and give it to someone in need.
40. Write a song that will uplift people.
41. Make it your goal to make 5 stranger's laugh, or smile.
42. Say I love you when you do.
43. Forgive people.
44. Do your best to not waste food.
45. If you are not already, become a hugger!
46. Sew, knit, or crotchet garments/blankets and donate them.
47. Reduce water waste.

48. Have a positive frame of mind (it is contagious and will bring joy to others)
49. When people are having a tough day, compliment them.
50. When spending time with people, give them you full attention with no distractions.
51. Deliver meals to new moms.
52. Respond to people when they reach out to you.
53. Purchase tickets to something recreational and donate them (swimming passes, ice skating passes, golf etc.)
54. Prioritize time with people you love. Put away electronics in their presence and don't use the excuse that you are too busy.
55. Do you constantly upgrade your computer or cell phone? Donate them to a community center.
56. Use reusable shopping bags.
57. Open doors for strangers.
58. Be conscious of purchasing fair trade items.
59. Don't give advice to people.
60. Don't judge others or criticize.
61. If you see someone in a crisis, offer a hand.
62. See a stranger visibly upset? Offer support.
63. Tell the people you love what is inspiring about them.
64. Tell jokes and be silly.
65. Offer your cooking/cleaning services to someone who could use a hand.
66. Thank people often and out of the blue.
67. Rid your negative thoughts. Your happiness is a gift to people you love.
68. Be a person who puts a positive spin on things.
69. Don't support social media that puts people down.
70. Consider a volunteer vacation.
71. Offer to care for animals while friends/family are away.
72. Buy and gift tickets to a comedy event for someone who needs it.
73. Take someone who is stressed out for pampering.
74. Give flowers (or anything) unexpectedly.

75. Write letters to people you love that are in gratitude to them. Mail them.
76. Try to be a zero garbage household
77. Call and let people know that you are there for them.
78. Do not try to change people. Love and embrace them as they are.
79. Cheer people on for who they are.
80. Write a thank you card to someone who inspires you.
81. Write a thank you note to someone who made a profound impact on you when you were young.
82. Write the Letter Series for someone you love and give it as a gift (pg. 154)
83. Print your favorite photo of you and a loved one. Frame it and write the loving memory behind the photo. Explain why it is special to you. Give it.
84. Gift and share music that makes you feel loved.
85. Offer a helpful hand indiscriminately and often.
86. Make jewelry with kind messages incorporated. Gift them to strangers.
87. Host an appreciation night for friends and family. Cook their favorite foods and serve their favorite beverages. Give a speech that honors all of your guests.
88. Ask people what they love?
89. Tell people what you love about them.
90. Share with people what you love!
91. Tell jokes to strangers while in line ups.
92. Write kind notes and put them on people's windshields.
93. Plug parking meters when they are low to help someone avoid a ticket.
94. Help people carry their groceries.
95. Offer to let people go ahead of when they seem rushed.
96. Make bagged lunches and include a loving note. Give them to people in need.
97. Stop using the word "should". Either do, or don't.
98. Be honest.
99. Teach someone Dani's Self-Love Meditation (page 92)
100. **Try the Glad Mail Challenge!**

Pat Armitstead
World's First Joyologist

New Zealand

My first contract in New Zealand was with a private training company. The attendance rates were 35% and so were outcomes. Not good!! The disciplinary process was to send 3 warning letters and then students were "dismissed." As the leader I refused to comply with this practice. You see, I knew this would not bring about change. The students were second chance learners from a poor area who got beaten up before they came to class! There was nothing motivating in these communications from the company.

So, instead I sat with every student. I sat with them until I knew them well enough to write them a one page letter. In that letter, I honored the good that I saw, the qualities I admired and the progress they had made. Sometimes their results were not great....but I discovered if you sit with people long enough you find out all you need to know. I was with that company two years and wrote 2000 pieces of personalized mail. When I left the attendance rate was 95% and so were outcomes. I wrote to and honored those who came and the word spread.

When I left I committed I would from that point on write 3 pieces of, what I call, "Glad Mail" every day. To date, I have sent well over 10,000 pieces of mail. Every presentation I give at conferences, I randomly hand out 3 pieces of Glad Mail written the night before based on what I intuit will be required by the person receiving.

Why would I do this?

From 1997 to 2001 I lost my home and business twice. I moved countries and arrived in NZ owing $80,000, which I repaid in 2 years. I had lost my first child, a daughter. I was also a cancer survivor. When I arrived in New Zealand I had ten car accidents, about 6 weeks apart! None my fault honest! My family had not spoken since 1989, and then my partner of 20 years left with another woman. I was devastated...his last words to me were "No, I don't love you and I never loved you!"

It was at that point I disintegrated. I thought if that is true then everything I know is not true.

I committed at that point that whatever came up in my life, I would go to it.

And then ... something began to happen. A chance conversation with a magician from South Australia and I had a huge revelation. I thought..." Oh my…we have radiology, pathology, and hematology …but no joyology! I am going to be a Joyologist. "

And so I became the World's First Joyologist.

I remained present and connected to my path and experienced so much paradox and synchronicity as the concept and my role evolved. I now have over 5000 testimonials that include this from **Dr. Ric Coleman,** *"Pat Armitstead is NZ's answer to Patch Adams."* I have also been likened to *"a spiritual midwife delivering people out of the darkness"*.

Where am I leading with this?

As I have evolved since 2001 I have committed over and over to refine and polish my language and to speak lovingly and authentically as my way of being. Now I see what that has attracted to me with so many wonderful words coming back from people who have enjoyed my presentations or my coaching. I was honored to speak at New Zealand's "Be the change you want to see" conference in 2000, and it has been a privilege to be a contribution to so many. I have lived my life with intention and my Glad Mail is one of my ways of expressing that.

Glad Mail Challenge

- Find at least one person each day who needs to hear from you; who needs your recognition and words of appreciation. Send them a letter, a card, a handwritten note, or an email.
- Keep a 30 day record of the glad mail you send and the feedback you receive.

MONTH

MY 30 Days of GLAD MAIL

SUNDAY	MONDAY	TUESDAY	WEDNESDAY	THURSDAY	FRIDAY	SATURDAY

Although THE SENTIMENT OFTEN SLIPS AWAY, TIME IS THE ECONOMY *of our lives.*

Love Buns

We all have those memories that seem brighter than the others. They are the ones that unexpectedly leap forth and linger a little longer. I always hold those memories a bit closer because I like to think these hold the lessons that we still need to learn. I honor them for the wisdom that seems to be confined within.

This is one of those memories:

As a little girl, I remember watching my mom in the kitchen. She moved quickly. At the time, I never really knew why, but looking back I realize that as a mother of 3 small children, close in age, running on high speed was simply a necessity. We have all juggled the clock: saving a few minutes here, adding a few more there, balancing life's "to dos" to somehow fit within our waking hours, so that we have some precious moments left to LIVE. Although the sentiment often slips away, time is the economy of our lives.

The fragrance of food has the amazing ability to transport us back in time, to a specific moment, to a particular place in our history, holding all of the feelings surrounding it. For me, the earthy, sweet, and spicy scent of cinnamon takes me to my childhood. It brings me back to my mom in the kitchen. Wherever I am, that smell gathers me close and overwhelms me with love.

While I am sure there are many more, I can only really recall two, maybe three occasions where the scent of cinnamon permeated the kitchen. The sweet, aromatic scent of her "Love Buns" seemed to linger for days. I am sure she would claim that is because that's how long it took her to make them. No special occasion, for no particular reason that I am aware of, she baked these cinnamon buns for my Dad. She renamed them "Love Buns" because she always said you really have to love someone a whole lot to spend that much time baking for someone. As children, we would always laugh at that… but now I understand.

Perhaps the greatest act of love is offering our time. We don't have the luxury of knowing exactly how much we have, but if we spend it acting in kindness, we have used it wisely.

Love Buns Recipe

DOUGH:

¼ cup white sugar

½ cup warm water

2 ¼ teaspoons active dry yeast

½ cup milk

1 teaspoon salt

2 eggs, beaten

4 cups (approximately) all-purpose flour

FILLING:

1 cup butter

1 ½ cups packed brown sugar

1 cup coarsely chopped pecans

1 tablespoon cinnamon

DOUGH:

1) Dissolve 1 teaspoon of sugar in warm water, sprinkle in yeast and let stand for 10 minutes or until frothy.
2) Meanwhile, in a small saucepan, heat the milk, remaining sugar, butter and salt. Warm until the butter melts. Allow cool until mixture becomes room temperature.
3) In a large bowl, combine eggs, milk mixture and yeast mixture.
4) Using an electric mixer, gradually beat in 1 ½ cups of the flour. Beat for 2 minutes, or until smooth. With a wooden spoon, gradually stir in enough of the remaining flour until the dough is soft, slightly sticky, and comes away from the dough.
5) On lightly floured surface, knead the dough for 7-10 minutes, or until it becomes smooth and elastic.
6) Place the dough in a large, butter-greased bowl. Turn the dough, so that the butter covers all of it. Cover with plastic wrap and let the dough rise for 1 ½ hours in a warm place (or in refrigerator overnight). The dough should be double in size and should retain impressions.
7) Punch the dough down.

FILLING:

1) In a saucepan over medium heat, melt the ¾ cup of the butter with ¾ cups of the sugar. Whisk until smooth.
2) Pour this mixture into a 13 X 9 inch baking dish. Sprinkle with ½ of the pecans and set aside.
3) Melt the remaining butter and set aside.
4) Combine the remaining sugar, pecans and cinnamon. Set aside.

Putting it together:

♡ On a lightly floured surface, roll out the dough into an 18 X 14 inch rectangle. Brush with 2 tablespoons of the melted butter leaving a one half inch border uncovered.

♡ Sprinkle with sugar mixture.

♡ Starting at the long side, tightly roll up, pinching the seam to seal.

♡ Cut into 15 pieces and place them in the pan, covered for one hour to rise (or until doubled in size).

Bake in a 375 degree oven for 25 to 30 minutes (until the crusts are gold and the tops sound hollow when tapped). Let stand in the pan for 3 minutes. Invert the pan onto a serving platter and scrape off the remaining filling and drizzle over the buns.

After you have done all that, you'll know why I renamed these cinnamon buns "Love Buns" 'cause you have to love someone a whole lot to make these for them!

LOVE GRAFFITI

CUT THIS PAGE ✂ DISTRIBUTE IN

RANDOM, PUBLIC LOCATIONS!

IT IS NO COINCIDENCE THAT YOU HAVE FOUND THIS. YOU ARE WORTHY.

IT IS NO COINCIDENCE THAT YOU HAVE FOUND THIS. YOU ARE BEAUTIFUL!

IT IS NO COINCIDENCE THAT YOU HAVE FOUND THIS. YOU ARE TALENTED!

IT IS NO COINCIDENCE THAT YOU HAVE FOUND THIS. YOU ARE WISE!

IT IS NO COINCIDENCE THAT YOU HAVE FOUND THIS. YOU ARE LOVED!

IT IS NO COINCIDENCE THAT YOU HAVE FOUND THIS. YOU ARE APPRECIATED!

love →

When
you give love
to the
universe,
That is what
is returned.

LOVE GRAFFITI
THE BOOK OF LOVE

LOVE GRAFFITI
THE BOOK OF LOVE

LOVE GRAFFITI
THE BOOK OF LOVE

LOVE GRAFFITI
THE BOOK OF LOVE

LOVE GRAFFITI
THE BOOK OF LOVE

LOVE GRAFFITI
THE BOOK OF LOVE

We can
not do
great
things.
We can
only
do little
things
with
great love.
-Mother Teresa

rethinking COMPROMISE

As we grow into a culture that embraces diversity and celebrates difference, naturally the act of compromise continues to flourish. We bend, shift, and change our wants, desires and journeys, in the hope of finding the idyllic middle ground. Our relationships with family, friends and spouses reflect the ideal that we can act, and think in a way that honors all parties involved. The common line of thought is that if one person bends their wants, hopes, or dreams, then the other can too, and this will result in the happiness of both parties involved. While this seems worthy of celebration, let me tell you a brief cautionary tale.

There once was a young man and woman who fell madly in love. They adored the time they spent together, and felt pure happiness in the presence of the other. They became inseparable. As time passed, friends and family began to nudge them into a marriage. As more time passed, the subtle hints became increasingly demanding. While the couple didn't see the need, they gave in and succumbed to the outside pressure. Everyone seemed happy and the decision seemed to prove positive. Soon, all of their friends began to buy houses and the couple followed suit. She hated cooking, but fulfilled her duty. He begrudged yardwork, but did it anyways. She loathed cleaning, but kept the house tidy. He loved socializing, but she didn't. Eventually, they stopped going out with friends. She was happy with that decision, but he wasn't. They could hardly afford their new home, but decided to work more to alleviate the financial pressure. As time passed, the wife tells the husband that she really wants children. Although the husband would rather wait, he compromises by agreeing. Once again, they need to work more to provide for their young child. As the years pass, the compromises compound and before the couple knows it, they are no longer themselves, nor had they stopped to ask themselves: Who am I? What do I want? What do I love? What am I really passionate about? Love turned into resentment and their relationship ended. They were living everyone else's dream except their own.

The sad truth is this fictional tale resembles many relationships. We do things that we don't want to because we don't want to hurt people. We don't do what we truly want because we fear the onslaught of judgement. We run our lives in a way that will gain the approval of our parents, loved ones, and friends. We trade ourselves for a socially approved creation. It is as though our rebellious adolescent spirit fatigues and we spend our remaining years *giving* in at the cost of ourselves. This will not ring true for everyone, thank goodness, but for those of you who connect with this, keep reading.

As youngsters, we are taught the meaning of cooperation and this evolves into our core understanding of compromise. We learn that giving our toy to a friend, or sibling is cooperating when truly all we want to do is play with it. We are rewarded for these acts of sharing and discouraged from selfish behaviors. Then as adults, we come to recognize compromise in the same way. It too becomes a celebratory pursuit. Unfortunately, too many of us compromise by means of giving up something that we really love because of someone else's desires. But wait, aren't we also taught that we should celebrate diversity? And this is exactly the heart of the issue. We have these two conflicting social ideals and most of us haven't' taken the time to resolve them. This isn't to say that compromise is bad… it isn't! But being agreeable should not be at the cost of yourself, your core values, or your integrity.

HOW TO COMMUNICATE COMPROMISE &

live your truth

First, honoring your truth is not selfish. Do your best to let go of the guilt of *letting people down*. At the end of the day, anyone who loves you will want you to be happy and that is up to you to define what that means. There is no *right*, or *wrong* when it comes to living your life. Rather, there is mainstream and alternative (unusual, odd, unconventional – use whatever antonym you choose). Your choices are right for you!

Decide in your mind what is uncompromisable and what subjects you are willing to bend with!

Use this scale to help you decide:

Definitely, no ---------------------Maybe --------------------Absolutely, Yes

0   5   10

0 = No Compromise

1-9 = Willing to Compromise

10 = No Compromise

Once you have made this decision in your mind, you can effectively communicate this with others.

"I will not compromise on this"

"I am willing to compromise (I am a 5, I am close to a non-compromise, I am very close to saying no/yes etc.)"

These clear statements will avoid miscommunication, wasted energy, and someone doing something that they really don't want to. For those who are in romantic relationships, you may want to share this scale with your partner. The more people who are communicating clearly, the better. This clarity is an act of self-love because you are preserving your truth. It is an act of giving love because you are sharing what you truly believe thus allowing others to be closer to your authentic self. This is the language of love! Keep in mind our truth is always evolving and not everything is negotiable. Just because you, or a loved-one felt uncompromisable in one scenario that is not say this is their "forever truth". Experience, time, and life changes us and our perspective. So check in often with yourself and those around you.

What to do when both Parties Feel Uncompromisable

For the Small Stuff:

I.e.: laundry, cooking, laundry, garbage (all household chores), vacations, delegation of holiday time, social events, entertainment time etc.

These issues do not really have the power to alter the course of a relationship. They may feel like big issues, but at the end of the day they are easy to resolve! If they do have a major impact, it is most likely due to miscommunication/clarity of communication.

Keep in Mind:

- ♡ Our opinions and the perspectives of others are always shifting. Don't make assumptions based on past answers. Check in often.
- ♡ Outsource! Do both members of a household hate cleaning? Hire someone! Can't afford it? Make a decision based on your reality, or change your reality.
- ♡ Both parties **can** get their way! Ask yourself, what is the possible resolution to this disparity? The middle ground can mean 2 people doing separate things.
- ♡ Respect the difference. Just because you feel one way, doesn't mean everyone else should. Honor your truth and the authenticity of others.
- ♡ It is okay to go separate ways for entertainment, passions, holidays, vacations etc.
- ♡ Ask yourself if you are being ridiculous. Are you not willing to compromise on something that really doesn't matter? There is a difference between stubborn and being authentic.
- ♡ Ask for clarification! What does the particular topic mean to the other person? Have you really thought about what it means to you? Share that.
- ♡ Be fluid. Allow your position to evolve on the small stuff!
- ♡ Own your position. Take responsibility for the results of your firm choices!

For Big Issues:

I.e.: marriage, place of residence, food choices, sex, spirituality/religion, career, children, lifestyle, body modification, education, health, acquisition of animals, future visions/goals etc.

These issues pose more of a challenge, but there is always a resolve. It may not be what you expected, but then again nothing is.

Keep in Mind:

- ♡ Communicate clearly what the word, or action means to you. Ask the same of the other person. Often, what we want, or don't want lies within the way we define it. We cannot assume our definition is universal because in all likelihood it differs from most. After clarifying, be willing to reposition whether or not you are willing to compromise.

- ♡ Have the appreciation that it may end the relationship as you know it. For example, if you really want to live in India and your partner doesn't, that could be a *deal breaker*.

- ♡ Understand the choices of another person do not, nor should they, reflect your thinking. If you don't want a dog, but your partner does and neither of you is willing to compromise, you can both get what you want. That is not your choice, it is theirs. They own the responsibility, but their choices are not a reflection of you.

- ♡ Respect the decisions. Your decisions are a reflection of you and nobody else. The same goes for any other party in your relationships. Does you dad want a tattoo and you are strongly opposed? No biggie! He gets one and you don't. You cannot control others, nor would you want to. Honor the individuality of others and let go of the illusion of control.

- ♡ Ask yourself if you are over-planning. Does there really need to be an answer now? Be okay with uncertainty because that is authentic. We cannot predict how we will feel in the future. Being certain is a false sense of security. It is utterly impossible and unreasonable to ask psychic abilities of ourselves, or those around us. How will you feel about this in 5 years? In truth, nobody knows.

- ♡ Respect the evolution of yourself and others. Just because you are unwilling to compromise one day, experience will naturally evolve your position. The same goes for others. It is rare (some would say undesirable) to be steadfast about everything.

JOURNAL, OR DOODLE YOUR
EXPERIENCES OF GIVING LOVE

No act of kindness is
ever wasted - Aesop

RECEIVE LOVE:

ALLOW THE

EXPERIENCE OF

LOVE

I looked in
temples,
churches,
and mosques.
But I found
the Divine within
my heart.
-Rumi

A Letter for You

It is no coincidence that your eyes have happened to stumble upon this text. The universe has collaborated to create this moment, the feelings, and the revelations that will arise within you. You are meant to be where you are at this moment reading the words that follow.

In case you haven't heard it in a while, or ever, I need you to know that you are talented. Contained within you is a wealth of gifts that you are meant to share. Know that you are far better than you have ever given yourself credit for. The script that you write within your mind does not compare to how extraordinary you really are. Too often, you see a false version of yourself that does not resemble the truth. You are not ordinary; you are a gift to this world. You were not meant to blend in; you are meant to shine. From now on, believe in your unique talents and allow them to flow from within you. When this happens, the world will become a more beautiful place because of you.

In case you haven't heard it in a while, or ever, I need you to know that you are beautiful. Your body does not parallel to another, so you really shouldn't compare it. It is magnificent in every imaginable way. Your skin tells a beautiful story that you should not hide. Every mark, scar and curve reveals a deep truth about you, where you have been, and who you are. Your body is the eclectic story of you and no detail is a mistake. Too often, when you look at your reflection, words wander within your mind that scribe untruths, and scar your soul. You are not flawed, you are perfectly beautiful. No other being appears the way you do and you are meant to hold your head high because of this. From now on, know deep within you that you are beautiful and exude pride because of that. When this happens, the world will become a more extraordinary place because of you.

In case you haven't heard it in a while, or ever, I need you to know that you are wise. Within your mind and soul, you have all of the answers you have ever needed. Know that regardless of how lost you sometimes may feel – this feeling is never real. In truth, it is an illusion that arises when you measure your path to another. You know your way, where you are going, and why you are here. Too often, you feel uncertain and look beyond yourself for solidity. Hear the words around you, but listen to the ones within you. Your mind is gifted and you are intuitive. Nobody else in the world has guidance for your journey because your path is yours to pave. You are not meant to wander their words; your steps are meant to mirror your soul. Each movement is an extension of your wisdom. From now on, know that caged within you is all of the wisdom you ever need. Allow the walls to fall and listen with trust. When this happens, the world will be a more magical than ever before because of you.

In case you haven't heard it in a while, or ever, I need you to know that you are worthy. All of the positive experiences in your life have appeared because you are deserving of them. No, it is not luck. When you exude joy, this is what has been drawn in your life. Too often, you do not give yourself credit. You are far more magnetic and deserving than you know. Every wonderful person, every smile, and all of those happy memories have happened because you are worthy. I need you to know that you deserve more than you are allowing to shape in your world right now. You deserve happiness in all facets of your life. The road is not meant to be rocky. You are worthy of your dreams coming true. From now on, know that greatness will happen to you in innumerable ways and it is because you are worthy. When this happens, the world will smile brighter because of you.

Thank you for being you, the world just wouldn't have been the same.

A Letter for You Series

You cannot always count on the support and love of others in the exact moments that you need it. Every once in a while you need a little more love in your life. And sometimes it is up to you to supply it.

The Writing Series

You will Need:

- 8 Envelopes
- ♡ 8 Sheets of Paper
- ♡ Glue/Scissors
- ♡ Writing Instrument of your Choice

The Task:

Write yourself 8 letters. It doesn't have to be all at once! Record the words on your envelope seals as the titles for each of your letters. You are wise and divine beyond what you acknowledge and this writing series celebrates that!

CUT THIS PAGE AND GLUE THESE LABELS ON

the flaps of your envelopes to seal them. Open your letters as required.

The Next Time
You are Alone &
Need to Celebrate,
Open this···

The Next Time
You are Alone &
Feel like Crying,
Open this···

The Next Time
You are Alone &
Feel Scared,
Open this···

The Next Time
You are Alone &
Feel Angry,
Open this···

WRITE OR DRAW 🎨 YOUR 3 WISHES

Date:

RELEASE YOUR WISHES

Too often we keep what we want most in the world locked up within. We keep our birthday wishes a secret in fear that if we share them they will not come true. We wish on stars, throw coins in wells, and hold our breath in dark tunnels in hopes that our deepest desires will miraculously manifest through our intent silence.

Break the Superstition of Silence! Share at least one of your wishes with anyone. Better yet, share all of them with everyone. Release exactly what you want into the universe and record the LOVE and support you receive.

Ask and you shall receive…

RECORD THE LOVE ♥ AND SUPPORT

you received below:

GRACIOUSLY ACCEPT

• •

We are nurtured to be independent beings. We are taught that we can do everything on our own and that is worthy of admiration. With this so-called strength comes the persisting comment, "no thank you. I can handle it myself." Of course you can! Assistance is not a reflection of your ability. It is an offer of love.

We decline the help of others because we don't want to burden them. We say no because we are stubborn. We reject these offers because we fear to appear incapable. We use our autonomy as proof that we *can* do it. We are fiercely independent because we feel unworthy of the support. Whatever your reason, remember this: love is reciprocal. The more you say no, the less people will offer. The less people want to help others, the less love there is in the world. Graciously accepting help is not just about you (which is immensely important), it has a real global impact. Receiving support is not selfish, in a sense it is selfless.

Haven't you ever had that experience of offering to help so often that it begins to feel like nagging? Your offers become sparser, or even slow to a stop. In school, some of us are taught to not open doors for physically challenged people because they are capable, and this offer diminishes their abilities. Really?! This thinking builds fear that helping others is offensive. Can't we just open doors for all people, indiscriminately with love?

We need to learn that:

- ♡ Strength isn't measured by how thin we wear ourselves down.
- ♡ Independence is measured by how lonely our struggle is.
- ♡ Pride isn't measured by how little we help we receive from others.

And if we can learn that, we can also learn to accept love.

The next time someone offers to assist you in any way, pause. Ask yourself if you would truly like to take them up on the offer. If you do, then graciously accept with gratitude.

THE 7 DAY AWARENESS CHALLENGE:

Keep

YOUR EARS OPEN FOR PEOPLE OFFERING ASSISTANCE, LOVE AND SUPPORT. TAKE THE EXTRA TIME TO THINK ABOUT WHAT YOU REALLY WANT. IF YOU FEEL LIKE DECLINING ASK YOURSELF WHY.

TAKE THE TIME TO EXPLORE HOW YOU REACT TO OFFERS OF SUPPORT.
RECORD EXAMPLES OF HELP YOU HAVE BEEN OFFERED.
WHAT WERE THE REASONS BEHIND YOUR ANSWERS?
WHAT CAN YOU LEARN FROM THIS?

Because one
accepts oneself,
the whole world
accepts them.
-Lao Tzu

Hidden within our response to compliments is something far deeper than modesty. For some of us, they cause an emotional stir, we look downwards, and even blush with embarrassment. Somehow, the compliments feel *above us*. Yet, most people share their genuine truth (it is not our job to discern the honesty of others). So, to save time and emotional energy, we can conclude that the compliments you receive ARE truth. These compliments are not above you, they are a mirror of some of the value you give in the world.

A. What is your physical reaction when people compliment you?
   Circle your typical response.

   Blush
   Look downwards or away
   Smile in nervousness
   Look shocked
   Feel Energized
   Look into their eyes
   Smile with a sense of pride
   Hold my shoulders back with confidence

B. What do you think, or say when you are given a compliment.
   Circle your response.

   Say, "thank you" but don't believe it
   Say, or think: no, not really, or I wish
   Say, "thank you" and believe it.
   Believe all compliments are a true reflection of you

   Review your responses: do need to make a shift?

SCRIBE ALL OF THE COMPLIMENTS YOU HAVE BEEN GIVEN THROUGHOUT YOUR LIFE.

CUT THEM AND POST THEM AROUND YOUR HOUSE FOR A WEEK.

Believe!

I am...

I am...

I am...

I am...

I am...

I am...

I am...

I am...

I am...

DO YOU SABOTAGE LOVE?

Many of us, maybe even you, have sabotaged love (we have both been there and done that)! Recognize the signs, and evolve to receive the love that you want and deserve.

Signs of Sabotage:

♡ Being totally different around different people. This is not to say that every person doesn't bring out a unique *side* to you, but you shouldn't have completely different personas. We always aim to be our whole person, to all persons. Ask yourself, "what do I hide about myself around_____?" "Am I being inauthentic to please others?" "Do I fear others will not like the real me?"

♡ Requesting, demanding, or disapproving of someone being their authentic selves. Have you ever asked someone to *tweak* who they are to be more compatible with what YOU want? This is sabotaging love. When we ask others to change their being, this is loving pieces of them and not their whole being. Aim to love everyone as they are…no *touch ups!*

♡ Avoiding, or not communicating your truth. I am sure there are many exceptions to this one, but if you are avoiding communication with loved ones because *it is not worth the conversation*, this topic is worthy of some thought. If you love someone, telling your truth is always worth the energy for all persons involved.

♡ Creating, maintaining, or not breaking down the walls around you. Do you truly let people in? Or, do you build precautionary walls to guard yourself from hurt? The truth is, we cannot control other people, or predict future pain, but if we don't want to let people in, then maybe it is time to let them go…Make a decision on whether it is your intuition, or past experiences blocking you from being vulnerable to love. Yes, love and life is a risk, but there is also a huge payoff. Take the lessons from the pain, and pride from the triumphs.

♡ Shifting your thoughts, being, or actions based on others beliefs. Ever had that experience of not doing something because you know someone else doesn't like that, or approve of that themselves? Instead of sculpting yourself to them, have pride in the masterpiece of YOU. A friend doesn't like tattoos and you love them? Flaunt them. They can leave you, or LOVE you (and that means all of you!)

- ♡ Allowing people to treat you like shit. Here it is: if someone treats you poorly (however you choose to define that), it is ONLY because you allow them to...Yes, that is a hard truth to swallow, but most of the time there are those particular *people* in our lives who hurt us mentally, emotionally, or spiritually and *we allow it*. It is possible to have zero criticism, zero judgement and one hundred percent compassion and love in your life. How? Communicate authentically, evaluate and honor your truth. Sometimes we evolve in different directions and that is okay.

- ♡ Nitpicking, or nagging. This is really strange, but it happens. Is your biggest contention with someone because they don't take out the trash? Do laundry? Put laundry in the basket? Keep a tidy room? Or, whatever? In our house, we either like to do it and do it, or don't like to do it, and don't. You can do only what you love. Do it, don't do it, or outsource, but don't complain. It is soooo not worth tainting love over dirty dishes!

- ♡ Finding a problem when everything is great. Do you look for ways to create an issue when there isn't one? Do you purposely act in an inauthentic way to drive someone crazy? Some of us find reasons to end, or sabotage love because we hold on to the belief that if everything is too good to be true, it is. This "seek and destroy mentality" will be effective. We do have the power to have problems when we want them, or embrace the love before us.

- ♡ Not actively showing, thinking, or acting in self-love. Do you skip your *"me time"*? Do you put yourself last? Do you not do the things that are integral to your being? What does this convey to others? If we give out the message that we love ourselves in a way that we should come last, then others could get the vibe that is what you want. Be sure to love yourself in a way that you take care of yourself emotionally, physically and spiritually. Don't forget that you are WORTH it.

- ♡ Purposely sabotaging instead of telling the truth. Are you destroying a relationship because you don't have the courage to end it? Have the courage to face your own truth and be honest! This type of sabotage is not fair for anyone involved. Did you once love someone and now don't? Make a decision.

THE LANGUAGE

OF LOVE:

A CELEBRATION

OF INDIVIDUALITY,

WISDOM

& EXPERIENCE

This is a celebration of individuality, wisdom and experience. Each story, explanation, and definition exemplifies the courage and vulnerability it takes to love, and to be loved. They serve to remind us all of its pure, yet complex nature. The words before you demonstrate that in times of adversity, strife, exultation, or bliss, the answer is LOVE. They show us that despite our divergent descriptions, the common thread of love binds all beings in our global community. There is no single answer to what love is. Love knows no age limits. Regardless of our roots, spirituality, religion, or individual gaze, we all have the capacity to love and be loved. May the words before you inspire internal change and evoke external action. Love is not reserved for a lucky few, love emanates from all. Let love liberate you from the confines of your being.

This is the era of love.

Love is being with someone and hugging them.
It is when you show someone
by kissing them.
You can't just say, "Hi, I love you!"
That's not very nice.
You should give them lots of love
and give them gigantic pictures,
or gigantic hugs!
Because love is something in your heart.
It feels nice because you get respected.
You don't get treated like you're stupid.
When you love someone, you try to be as nice
as you can to respect them back
when they are respecting you.

Kayla, Age 5

Love is such a powerful word, powerful emotion, powerful tool.

It can be defined in so many different ways, it can have so many different meanings to different people. But it all stems from one thing… spirit. Love is the only one thing that is truly real. It exists from within our emotions, our feelings; it is our root, it is the only reality of life, for all other things are made up in our thoughts. Stress, anxiety and worry all stem from fear – the opposite of love. Fear is false evidence appearing real and love is the light that overpowers fear just as the candle overpowers darkness.

We are born from love, with love and to love. Love is everywhere just as God is everywhere. We all seek love and we all yearn to be filled with this emotion that keeps us alive. We would not have survived without it since the day we were born. As I birthed three children, each and every time my newborn arrived into this world, ever so precious, every breath of life of theirs is every breath of life of mine. Their heartbeat inside of me forever is the music that I dance to in life. The love of a mother to the newborn child, as this gift from God is brought into our arms, the love that has been bonded for nine months is the strength that is passed on to the mother that will love, cherish and care for every minute, every hour, every day, every night, week, month and year carrying and growing this love more and more from infancy, to toddler, to child, teen and adult. The cycle of love passes on forever more.

Love is the divine and when we allow ourselves to freely live from within, which is the divine source of love from which we were created, we learn to love ourselves, to love all and to love life. When we make the decision to live from this place and to send love we are in the flow of the divine Universe and how it is perfectly orchestrated. We free ourselves from the prison that holds us hostage when we live from our ego rather than our true divine self. We become free when we love those who we have forgiven, we love everyone that crosses our path, because we are all one, and so if we do not love even those who have hurt us, we are not loving ourselves, and so we block the divine flow of the purest energy of love to immerse within us. To love thy neighbor is to love oneself and to love thyself is to love thy neighbor.

We must give what we want to receive and so if we want to receive love, we must give love. To receive forgiveness, compassion and understanding we must give the same to others. The source of love is what brings light to darkness, brings joy to sorrow and brings healing to suffering. Love is the most powerful and healing tool that we are born with, but yet so many of us let it slip away and we no longer allow ourselves to be in tune with the most beautiful rhythm of the Universe… Love. You are love, therefore you must do whatever it takes to return to your true self, your spirit, your soul. That is where it is deep rooted.

The ultimate love is the love of life in itself, for if we love life, the love is returned to us by the things we do and by the people we surround ourselves with. There is no greater feeling than being surrounded by a circle of friends and family that brings joy and laughter and yet at the same time has the same loving surroundings during times of challenge, for it is their loves that empowers us and gives us strength. The divine love that exists in each and every one of us can bring forth miracles, laughter, joy, peace and healing. May you reconnect with the divine in you and let the light of love shine forth to everyone forever more.

Marilyn Ocasio
Founder of
Helping Heal
Hearts

IF WE WANT
TO BREAK THE CYCLE
of violence,
we must first have
the courage
TO SPEAK

Emotions are our body's reaction to personal experiences, our perceived reality. Conditioned responses come only after mental discipline and the acceptance of truth.

Not an easy undertaking, however well worth choosing to do.

I would learn by age nine that I was not what my mother wanted. Sexual abuse began by a close relative just a year later. *Who would I tell? Who would care? SILENCED!*

BEING REJECTED BY FAMILY IS THE DEEPEST BETRAYAL.

A soul cries to be loved, nurtured, heard, understood and above all, protected.

I had to become numb. I would soon realize I was good at domestic things, music and athletics. I could never do/be enough to silence the screams of my pain. I became the classic over achiever while continually feeling like an epic failure. Enter the mask of denial, it was far easier wearing the mask than revealing the broken version of me. In this choice, I denied my own truth, thus robbing me of years of healing and trust. As a result I have spent the whole of my existence searching for a safe, loving place, never feeling worthy and often sabotaging many would be successes. My heart ached for acceptance in love.

When the road rises up to meet you and smacks you square in the face, it is important to pay attention!

This time something drastic had to happen inside of me. These past five years have pushed me beyond any limits I thought possible, certainly with more plot twists, winding roads and demolished bridges than I could have ever imagined. I was forced to let go of so much and yet it was in the letting go that I found me! I found new doctors and a proper diagnosis thus liberating my body allowing my mind to once again function. Finally, I was being heard. With a clarity not experienced in years I found a new world of people, places and things.

Although at times I was mentally absent I have never been alone, I have had the **enduring love** of my husband, children, grandchildren, friends with whom I have spent countless hours navigating life. In a world of fast paced deletion human beings become mere counts on a social media page. This revolving door of acceptance and rejection is hollow and destructive. People are not disposable and life naturally purges people places and things. Be grateful for all who entered and learn from what you have allowed.

Many have helped heal my brokenness. Those that endured never wavered or looked for an easy way out. **Enduring love**, comes along side and reaches back in time and begins to unravel all the lies and pain. Each person along the way provided something, some were towers of strength providing gentle places to fall and safely hide while others delivered difficult truths and timely words of wisdom. The hardest part is recognizing this type of love as it is never boastful nor proud. Do not take it for granted, rather allow it inside your heart to help with repairs and healing.

I am humbled beyond measure for the **enduring love** that surrounds and supports me. I now embrace truth and no longer allow those who carelessly tossed around my life the power to crush me. Their selfishness will no longer dictate my actions nor silence my truth.

Don't mistake the depth of my emotion for weakness, rather try to understand the magnitude of my journey. Although I have freely given love, it is the love of the people who endured that speaks to me here and now. They have courageously traveled with me and have wrapped me in healing **enduring love** that has set me free.

I want to thank each of you who have chosen to stay the course; for showing up and living your role in the archeological dig of my life. I am in awe that through it all you saw the real me all along. On this side of the pain, I see how broken I was and because of your **enduring love**, I am learning to see and love me too. I am finally able to let go of the anger and rage of a childhood lost long ago. I choose the path of hope that I know will bring me comfort and finally peace.

WE all MATTER!

There is no scale or competition for pain nor prizes given for suffering. Love that endures the test of time heals the deepest pain.

What are you willing to let go of?

What are you willing to fully embrace?

Let love set you free, invite it in. It really is your choice.

Robbin King
Founder of Ameliorations:
Enhancing Daily Living
Age: 51
Denver, Colorado

Love is doing the things that make
you the most happy and being
with the person that makes you
the most happy.
It is the one feeling that you get
inside you that you will
always remember.
Love is a part of most
of our memories
and will always
stay with us.
Taylor
Age 13

In modern-day American culture, we seem to use the word "LOVE" and its most recognizable symbol "♥" for all kinds of things. A few examples: I ♥ pizza . . . I ♥ my phone . . . I ♥ my job . . . I ♥ that movie . . . I ♥ "this" and I ♥ "that." Do we really LOVE or are we just "in love" with the <u>word</u> "love?" Is LOVE in the DETAILS?

There are things I intensely like, however, nearly everything I LOVE is now or once was a living entity, be that plant, animal or human. I love my family. I love the many wonderful friends that bless my life. I love animals, flowers, plants, and the breathtaking beauties of nature.

As a Christian, I love my Heavenly Father and His Son, my Lord and Savior, Jesus Christ. In addition, the better I come to know them through studying their words and deeds, learning about them and talking with them in prayer, the greater my love for them grows. That they love me—and each of us individually—and express that love daily is nothing short of miraculous! Their LOVE for us is in the DETAILS."

In the Greek language, there are express terms for differing types of love. I like this; it lessens confusion and helps us understand the various levels and/or meanings of love. The Greek word "*storge*" denotes affection, familiarity, and can include love for our pets; the word "*philia*" indicates friendship between people sharing common interests; "*Eros*" represents two people being in love; and "*agape*"

signifies unconditional love especially as it relates to deity. Noted author C.S. Lewis expounds on these differing aspects in his work, *"The Four Loves."*

A picture in our home portrays these beautiful words:

> Love is patient; Love is kind; It is not arrogant or rude. Love does not insist on its own way; It is not irritable or resentful; It does not rejoice at wrong but rejoices in the right. Love bears all things; Believes all things; Endures all things. Love never fails (1 Corinthians 13:4-8).

In addition, a caring friend recently shared these meaningful thoughts: "Love is a way of life; Love is comfort; Love is a saving force; Love is an indicator of our priorities; Love is a motivator; Love is a commandment."

Inspiring and uplifting as all these words about love may sound, they are just that—words—unless we choose to make LOVE an integral part of our daily lives. Love isn't always easy; it requires on open heart and often takes work, commitment, determination, and selflessness. We can observe kind and loving people everywhere; perhaps by recognizing their actions we can improve our own.

Unlike the movies, love isn't limited to a breathless "I *love* you," romantic roses or a box of delectable chocolates—delightful as those may be! Many of the less dazzling, yet wonderfully heartfelt expressions of love that I value include kind words, tender kisses (including softly blown ones), cheerful smiles, friendly hugs, sincere listeners, short notes and caring phone calls. Add to that, personal visits, a plate of tasty treats or the sharing of beautiful flowers—including children's golden dandelions! Equally appreciated . . . one who grieves with those who mourn or who delights in the happiness of others. Often, these loving actions have such significance because they mean being there for someone when it is *not* convenient—when they (or we) had other plans. Of course, this list might continue endlessly. Each of us will show our love for others in differing ways; once again, LOVE ~ it's in the DETAILS.

Children often display love in sweet and gentle ways. Recently, our granddaughter spent a long weekend with us. She <u>loves</u> kitties. In addition to our house kitty, we have several barn cats that we feed; two of which are younger kittens. She lovingly fed and cared for them and would sit quietly for the longest time watching them eat, play and nap in the warm sunshine. Without being asked, she tidied up the area where they came to eat, carefully washed their food dishes and *secretly* spoiled them with kitty treats! She demonstrated her loving affection for them "in the details" of her caring actions.

Another day, with dollars she had worked hard to earn, this same dear one purchased, as a special treat for her, a chocolate dipped ice cream cone. Then — thinking more of others than her money — used the remainder to buy a chocolate dipped cone for someone else. When her Papa and I mentioned to her that she had just spent all she had, she smiled brightly and said, "Not all of it, Gramma, I still have 25-cents!"

LOVE ~ It's in the DETAILS!

Margie Kawamoto
Loving Mother
& Wife
Age 67
Washington, USA

You can love someone who does not even love themselves and you can love someone when all you get from them is hate. Love is a feeling that you have in

Love is something you feel even if it is not returned.

your heart but sometimes it may not even be on your mind. You can love people while they are here and still love them after they are gone. I think of my mother almost every day and am always happy to tell someone something about her. I have so many good memories of her. That is not to say that we did not have our disagreements. Or that she never made me angry because she did. I'm sure I made her angry many times too. But, I loved her so much and am so proud of her to this day.

My gratitude extends to all who have touched my life in positive and loving ways. I feel like I am surrounded by loving and kind people and I try to be around them as much as possible. My church family is so very important to me and I wish I could name all of the ones I love. I see them and I hug them and kiss them and wish them well with (as Dr. Connie says) a Good God Bless You! Those that I do not know I make an effort to go up to and introduce myself and find out their names. If the names are difficult I tell them that I may have to ask again (maybe five or six times) but eventually I will remember.

Smiles are so beautiful and hugs are so warm and so needed. I need to be around warm, sweet people to help make my day. I try to watch television programs that make me smile and enlighten me, like Steve Harvey's show and Family Feud. That helps make my day feel complete. I look for something to smile or laugh about. I love jokes and I love telling them. Whenever I try to rest, my mind goes to a luncheon that I have been invited to perform for and I think of things that will make the ladies laugh. I really am looking forward to the event. I smile at the thoughts I have and can't wait to get with my friend, Sandra so that we can mingle our thoughts. I hope so much that it goes well. I have memories of times when the performance was so well received and persons talked about it for months afterward, bringing smiles to my face and good thoughts about what it might be like next time. I truly am grateful.

Patty P.
Mother, Wife,
Grandma,
Great-Grandma
Age 73
Michigan, USA

Love is not about external appearance, or how much money someone has. It is about mutual respect and understanding. It is about accepting a person wholeheartedly .It is something we can see in other person's eyes. It is looking after each other in times of distress. Love is understanding each other without words.

Jaya Bhardwaj
Mother of 2,
Devoted Wife in an
Arranged Marriage
Age 51
Delhi, India

LOVE IS A VERB. LOVE HAPPENS IN ACTION.

Love, for me, is defined in the saying:

TO SEE A PERSON'S IMPERFECTIONS AND LOVING THEM FOR IT.

To this day I call him "my favorite mistake". One I'd repeat for the lesson I learned. He taught me the importance of being more mindful and pragmatic in love so as to choose wisely.

Jakob opened my shutdown heart after a long slumber of imprisonment. He showed me that I didn't have to be a slave to negative reactions in response to rejection, betrayal, and abandonment. Thanks to him, I learned that I can love a person deeply and authentically enough, to not even think to resort to such angry behavior.

Jakob approached me one summer night in San Francisco. I instantly recognized the familiar New York accent that always made me miss the East Coast. Since moving to California I had yet to fall to love on the West Coast. Jakob changed all that. Meeting him was pure synchronicity. That same evening I had participated in a BodyTalk workshop taught by my friend Lyn Delmastro. The topic of the seminar was "Fizzle to Sizzle". In an instant my love life was exactly that.

There were countless "I love you" moments from him. When he was in New

York, we would Skype or text often. There was an ease being with him. Jakob felt familiar from the start. I didn't have butterflies, head buzzing or heart racing sensations when we were together. Like Loving Relationship Expert Tamara Green, LCSW once described, it was a kind of acoustic attraction rather than an electric one.

We were total opposites. Jakob was athletic, had been an investment banker on Wall Street, spoke German, grew up on the Upper East Side, private school educated, and a Navy veteran. I was born and raised outside the US, preferred intellectual salon discussions, hated working out, and was very selective when I socialized. Our differences didn't divide us. Rather, the division of his mind did.

Jakob confided to me that he had been on anti-depressants since his divorce six years earlier. In the fall he began going a week or two without medication. He was erratic, seemed forgetful, irritable, and constantly changed plans. I knew work stress was not the sole cause and hoped it would pass.

On my birthday he was in Chicago for work but wouldn't set a date to celebrate. In frustration I said not to bother. Jakob called when he was back in town to tell me of a life altering decision he was making. He said he wanted to be in my life but geography was an issue. I felt crushed and ended things.

A month later, I got a faint positive result on a home pregnancy test. A girlfriend suggested contacting Jakob before getting a blood test to confirm pregnancy. Reluctantly, I did. He called immediately. Jakob said he got a dream job in Switzerland and couldn't fly back to California.

My friends provided the emotional support I really needed because it turned out to be a "chemical pregnancy". The fertilized egg implanted but didn't develop. My doctor said my body would expel the tissue naturally and I took bioidentical creams to rebalance my hormones. Jakob continued to ask to see me by Skype, saying he was either in Europe or New York.

Then I learned the truth when an email was undeliverable. Google mail server indicated that the IP of the server it bounced off of belonged to his gym in San Francisco. When I mentioned it to a techie girlfriend she determined that all his emails originated from a local IP server. She believed he had likely been local the entire time he said he was in Europe. The only truth was that he left the firm he worked at.

It all made sense. Jakob never sounded enthusiastic or gave details about his job in Switzerland.

I was shocked. Even after the pregnancy scare was over, Jakob asked me, "What can we create from here? You can see right through me and I feel we have such a strong connection". Now everything felt like a lie.

I didn't lash out. I simply blocked him from contacting me. All trust was destroyed. Only love remained but from a distance. My roommate said that his actions had nothing to do with me. I repeated those words like a mantra.

The Dalai Lama said, "*Sometimes not getting what you want is a remarkable stroke of good luck*". I couldn't agree more and have Jakob to thank for teaching this valuable lesson. For that, I have nothing but gratitude for him.

Charlotte Harcing-Soignee
Project Manager
Age 34
California, USA

LOVE IN MARRIAGE

My definition of Love in Marriage is how you and your partner feel toward each other. How you show each other you care. It is the deep affection that resonates deep within your heart and soul. Love is acts of kindness to each other. Love is all the gifts you give each other.

Love is how you speak to each other with compliments. Love is all the time you spend together and going on dates. Love is in all the hugs and kisses and physicality in a loving tender way.

Love Never Gives Up! 1 Corinthians 13:7

To my Beloved Husband Paulo:

Where do I start my darling, but at the beginning of our love. It was late on a summer night in a popular nightclub that the Love of God and our stars in alignment that brought us together. I prayed for you. Who could resist the handsome young man in the suit? Even now thinking of it brings tears to my eyes. How handsome you were that night. But deeper than your looks, you were funny, charming and generous. Of course being European and Portuguese was the clincher. Having grown up Italian, I always wanted a life partner that shared my culture, values, religion, hopes and dreams. We had so much fun dancing that night. Our relationship was strong from the beginning. I really enjoyed getting to know you and your family during those early days. We started as friends and as time went on we grew to love each other.

When you asked me to marry you and you sold your car for the engagement ring I knew I would always be your love. Any man who sells his car for a lady is a man worth keeping. You promised to take care of me and you have never broken your promise. You have taken good care of me. I also saw how much you love your mom and sisters and knew that any man who loves and cherishes his mom as much as you do would love his wife with reckless abandon. How blessed we are Paulo. We have always taken our vows seriously. We have had more good than bad. We have had more joy than sorrow and when I went through the cancer it was with the strength that God planted in you that you were able to take such good care of me. It was the love in your heart and soul that I felt and was able to keep me going on days where I thought I would surely die from being so sick. It was the love in your hands that massaged my weary chemo-riddled body back to health. It was holding my hands on days I had to be 8 hours on chemo. I flourished during that time with your love. I know it was a deep soul love for me that enabled you to garner all that strength it took to work and also take on all the household duties that I couldn't complete and in order to keep our business running smoothly.

It was all the love in you that carried us through our son's illness-epilepsy and all the seizures that were manifested during my illness.

Yes my love, we have been blessed by and with love. Our relationship is rich and abundant because of all the love that we share. In our family, love means that we spent holidays with our extended members of the family on both sides. Love meant we shared milestones in celebration. Love also meant we mourned together when one of our own returned to Heaven. Love meant that we helped brothers and sisters through divorces and deaths. We also had enough love to help friends who needed a hand up during difficult situations in their lives such as fundraising or job loss.

In our family love meant we always helped each other. We share our abundance with everyone we know. WE have parties and are generous and kind and

perform many random acts of kindness. Through our love we can give to the poor.

Love is also deciding to have a family and having a wonderful son and raising him with all the love of family values, time, compassion and being a caring human being. We lead by example. Love always being the root. Love is hugging, kissing, talking and sharing. Love is also speaking to each other with respect even though we may have human moments and yell sometimes. Love is our yearly camping trips. Love is our dog Bella. Love is taking care of her.

My darling, the love you show us is evident in how hard you work to provide for us. Love is how you provide us with all the necessities of life and so much more. Love is how dedicated you are to the family. To all of the family. My side and your side.

Oh my dear husband, when I reminisce over the past 30 years I see how LOVE got us through all the times we had something tough come up. I see how we have grown. WE have learned how the power of love is the strength to get us through it all.

You have such a good attitude. You always smile and are respectful. You work so hard. You never let much get you down and you have a deep knowing that only an old wise soul possesses.

We have so much to be grateful for. I remember on our wedding day when Father George gave us our matrimonial candle. He told us to light it and remember our special day if we ever felt lost and in need of extra light in our marriage. We should be very proud that that candle is as perfect as the day of our wedding. We have only lit it once in celebration!!!

My dear Paulo, my letter to you wouldn't be complete without my thanking you for always supporting me during my spiritual enlightenment
and my quest to heal myself. I am on a mission to stay in wellness and to be healthy. I want to be the best me I can be. I have learned to love myself first so

that I can love you and Paulo Jr. even more than I do already. These 30 years have been an amazing journey of love, perseverance, acceptance and mostly of growth. We really have grown up together. What a great example of love we are.

I look forward to the next phase of our marriage and of our life together. I hope God blesses us with a long healthy happy abundant life. I know the strength and depth of our love. I know with God's help we can get through whatever may come.

We have endured earth school with so much love. We know love is where we came from, who we really are and where we return. Love allows us to smile and be grateful through all of life and its lessons.

I pray that God blesses our marriage and our life with abundant health for I know health is wealth! Dear God thank you for my husband Paulo. My precious husband, I hope you know how loved you are. Don't ever forget it.
All my love... forever.

Giuliana Melo

Mind, Body,
Spirit Practitioner
Age 50
Alberta, Canada

Love is acceptance and understanding.
It is how you accept the other person
for whatever and whoever they are.
You don't care about their past.
You care about their present.
It is how you accept their true identity
and the quality of life he/she has.
It is how also you understand them
when a problem arises. You choose
to be with each other
no matter what.

Arl Paña
Age: 20
Davao, Philippines
The son of very
supportive parents
and a Boyfriend of a
far away Bangladesh man

Love is what our souls are made of.

WE ARE BORN TO LOVE - FRIENDS AND ENEMIES ALIKE.

It is instilled in us, we're pre-programmed. Unlike other emotions, love is not learned by watching and imitating others. We crave love from the moment we leave the womb. It is the emotion that most determines who we are, how we feel, how we act and react.

But as we grow, we learn negative emotions -such as anger and hate. The resulting negativity is nothing more than a sopping wet blanket that serves to extinguish the burning fire of love that lies within each of us.

There are many faces of love, both good and bad. The best love that I've experienced is unconditional love. And I never fully understood that, until I had a child of my own. There's nothing I wouldn't do for my son.

And now, despite all of my flaws and my countless mistakes, I know how much my parents truly love me. At thirty-six years of age, I cannot find the words to adequately express my gratitude for their love. To have two people in my life who love me wholeheartedly, without conditions or reservation, is something I hope everyone has a chance to experience for themselves. And lesson learned: I probably wouldn't have appreciated the magnitude of that love without having a child of my own.

If we could all learn to let go of expectations and conditions, loving would be so much more enjoyable and forthcoming. However, society has molded us in such a way that we're inclined, instead, to build walls. We view vulnerability as a sign of weakness, we require conditions and expectations.

We meet someone and fall in love, only to find out that the relationship was doomed from the beginning. In return, we aren't loved equally; or at all for that matter. Instead of parting as friends and being grateful for the experience, we become vindictive enemies. Hate then consumes us, and we're left "picking up the pieces" of our broken hearts.

Sure, love can cause pain. And that's because we've added the complexity of expectations. We're left broken and depressed, mourning the loss of a relationship that wasn't supposed to fail. Our self-worth takes a hit, and more often than not it takes a while to recover and get back on our feet.

I've had a few relationships that just didn't work; but I'd hardly consider them failures. I have learned many valuable lessons from them which I will carry with me for the rest of my life.

Although one relationship was horrible, I now know the early warning signs of simmering anger and the violence that follows. And my marriage came to an end, but I now know the value of communication. I've also learned that the little voice in my head screaming "I'm right and you're wrong!" is my ego trying to take charge. But because of these learned lessons, I now know how and when to silence it.

By opening up to all these people (family, friends, partners) throughout my life, I have learned both wonderfully beautiful and terribly ugly lessons - but lessons nonetheless. Love isn't always pretty. And sometimes, it's even going to hurt. But it's been said that pain can be our greatest teacher.

It's okay to be vulnerable, and open the door to the possibility of such pain. We can't live life to the fullest if we aren't learning along the way. And we can't let the <u>fear</u> of pain keep us from doing what we were born to do.

The world needs more love. And if we could learn to forgive and be grateful for what we have, or simply appreciate an experience, there would be far less animosity. People would begin to appreciate all that they possess within themselves, and the countless possibilities that lie ahead. Somewhere along the line, we've forgotten that we are as significant as we are.

You can't truly love someone else, if you don't love yourself first. But it seems that self-love has been thrown to the curb. Recognize and acknowledge your value, and be grateful for the experiences of this lifetime. No matter what the current circumstances are, much better things are on the way. We just need to change our perception, get rid of expectations and conditions and love everyone as our equal. I hope I live long enough to see that actually come about. Like any growing thing, love needs to be nurtured. If it isn't "watered," our population will surely die off rather quickly, swept away by waves of anger, hate and negativity.

Kate McKie

Mom, Writer
Forever Optimist
Age 36
New York, USA

Love is a thing where people take care of you. It means people care about you and like you. It feels nice to be loved because it means that people have you in their heart. I feel love in my heart and my body. It feels wonderful. You know somebody loves you because they could have smiles, eye contact, hugs, and kisses Hearts are as big as a fist and fists are big. So, we have a lot of room in our heart.

Jake, Age 7

TO LOVE ALL IS TO BE VULNERABLE.

— *C. S. Lewis* —

In Loving memory of
Kelcey Wayne Sullivan.
In the arms of the angels.

The beauty of love is it gets defined through unique life experiences.

THE BEAUTY OF LIFE IS LOVE CHANGES AND LIFE CHANGES.

I never knew the depth of love until I had to say goodbye. A forever goodbye. A life changing goodbye.

It was a November Sunday morning. A new sunrise. A new day. When the phone rang, a new journey had begun. The beginning of forever had started.

I knew this wasn't going to be a good call because it was an early morning call. I answered, "Hello?" The trembling voice on the other end was one I spoke to every day but this time, I barely recognized the voice. It sounded terrified, quivering, barely able to get the words out. The one thing we had in that moment was love. Love endures all and this call defined the "true love" of our family.

It was my mom on the other end. She said, "Kelcey has been taken to the hospital by ambulance. He's unresponsive and not breathing." My world shattered. I couldn't breathe. My hand rushed to cover my mouth as I gasped to breathe. The tears flooded down my face. All I could utter was, "I'll be right there."

Love was all we had in that moment. Love was all we knew in that moment. Love was all we could rely on in our prayers at that moment.

The hour and a half drive to the hospital seemed endless. When I arrived at the Emergency Room, I told the ER nurse whom I was there to see. She gently said,

"You can have a seat in the family room" and she escorted me to a brown door on the left. There sat my parents. Grief, horror, shock and disbelief filled the room but love kept us together.

The Coroner entered the room. He spoke foreign words to me to help explain what had happened; Murder, Homicide, Investigation. My brother was gone forever and I knew life had changed forever. In that moment, I was grateful for family love.

Staci York Hufty
Loving Sister
Age 44
Indiana, USA

To love someone unconditionally we
must be able love ourself first.
It is only when you can accept yourself
with your faults, that you can
love someone else with their faults.
To love someone is wanting the
best for them and not you.
This is truly difficult, as it
might mean letting go and it
can be scary. It is also freeing to know
that if they are meant to stay in
your life they will find a way on
their own free will.
True love is what love is meant to be.

Corinne Herbu-Louise
A woman, mother of 4
Age 39
Victoria, Austrailia

Love is one of the most powerful things,

IF NOT THE MOST POWERFUL THING IN THE WORLD.

Love is one of the most powerful things, if not the most powerful thing in the world. It is an emotion that is like no other. When you love something or someone, you feel as if you would do anything for them. It's truly a magical feeling that everyone deserves to experience. Though I am young, I have had many experiences with love.

There are different types of love: from the love you receive from your family, or the love from friends, to the love you receive from someone special. I can say this from personal experience that to receive love, you must give love and be open to new experiences.

The love you get from your family is unconditional. Sometimes things get tough, and life kicks you in the ass. You may feel very alone, but your family always loves you, regardless of your decisions, or mistakes. Your friends can bring so much love, or drama into your life. Your true friends will always be there for you through your struggles and adventures. Another type of love is admiration you have for someone special. When someone like this comes into your life, it feels your whole world has changed. This person can understand you like no one can. When you talk to them it feels like you're in a dream because it seems like it's too good to be true.

There are many misconceptions about love. My favorite one is love is easy. That's one of the biggest lies I have ever heard! Love is not easy, it is a big challenge, especially relationships. Loving someone is easier said than done. There's always so much drama about it. Sometimes I feel like why can't you just love anyone you want without drama, or judgement? There is always ups and downs in relationships, and not just romantic relationships. I have gone through points of my life where challenges have appeared in my relationships with friends and family. When it's with family it's hard, because sometimes when you need a break from them you can't get away and you feel trapped. It feels like you can't escape. This is one of many challenges that comes with loving someone.

I've had times where I have doubted the idea of love and didn't believe in the power it had on people. I've learned even through the darkest of times you can still find something, or someone to love. I have also learned that there is always someone out there that loves even when it feels like you have no one. The most important thing that I've learned throughout my life to open up to the idea of giving love and being loved, and it has impacted my life more than you could ever think.

Hunter
Age 14
Canada

WE ALL HAVE
THE POWER
TO ACT IN WAYS
THAT WILL
SPREAD LOVE
WHEREVER
WE GO.

The Language of Love

Use your Voice and Words To:

- ♡ Appreciate without seeking it in return
- ♡ Imagine without expectations
- ♡ Dream without constraint
- ♡ Share optimism without pesimism
- ♡ Spread knowledge without predjudice
- ♡ Value all beings without discrimination
- ♡ Express love without fear
- ♡ Honor truth without contention
- ♡ Embrace the authenticity of others without judgement
- ♡ Lift people higher without looking down
- ♡ Seek clarification without first assuming
- ♡ Encourage communication without presumption
- ♡ Aim to inspire without self-doubt
- ♡ Learn without regret
- ♡ Celebrate diversity without selectivity
- ♡ Promote positive action without obligation
- ♡ Admire without nerves
- ♡ Create beauty without discretion
- ♡ Praise courage without concern
- ♡ Encourage spritual growth without suggestions
- ♡ Inspire excellence without doubt
- ♡ Give compliments without apprehension
- ♡ Love all without reason

When you do all that, you have a language of love...

The amount of LOVE in your world begins with you...

The way you love yourself teaches others how to love you. YOU set the standard. So, set that bar high. Not because you're selfish, but because you deserves *that* kind of love. You deserve to be adored, respected, and celebrated by EVERYONE that surrounds you. Communicate your truth and don't compromise your authenticity for anyone. You and your dreams are non-negotiable. Act on those dreams. They are meant to be LIVED and not just within the confines of your mind. They are not farfetched. All is possible if we believe it to be so. Harness the courage to abandon the social ideals that you don't agree with and create a life you REALLY love. Wisdom presides within you. Listen to the quiet whispers within before they are silenced to the cries that surround you.

The way you give love is a mirror of your heart. Offer up that kindness, compassion and empathy to all. You have more than enough to give. It will not run out, it will replenish as needed. No need to justify, because *you yearn to* IS ample cause. Act on what pulls at the strings of your heart. And let the sound soar far and loud. Fear not what happens beyond that, for this is your song. There are no requirements to those who deserve love. Strangers need not be outsiders. Be that reason that makes someone smile. Be that person who gives generously without looking for something in return. Love and happiness are contagious and that can begin with you. You can be the seed of change by acting on what seems missing in your mind. All great change begins with one. And that one can be you.

The way that you embrace incoming love sends a message to the universe. Open your arms wide. Welcome love into your life the same way that you would welcome money. Don't turn your back to it, refuse it, or throw it away. Accept it as the Victorians did, with a curtsy and gracious words of gratitude. You are not too high, nor too low to accept love into your life. Each of us is on level ground, so let's lift each other higher. Let's rise with one another. Not in competition, but as equals. Receive love in the same way as you give it. Smile at the cheers and steer clear of being bashful. You are not a cause, you are THE cause of the love that surrounds you.

The way you speak is the sounds of your soul. Let it reverberate all of the goodness within you. Be whole and allow your language to reflect the love that you have within you. Speak kindly of others even if they don't speak kindly of you. There is a reason to compliment ALL beings, even if no one else does. You set the standards of your surroundings. Watch the gossip subside when you stop participating. See the love grow as you step forth with a loving language. As the negative language falls to the floor, the loving language will rise from the ashes. Love will rise as the sun does. It will shine bright, brilliant and will fall onto all beings IF you begin with you...

LOVE IS A VERB.
Act.

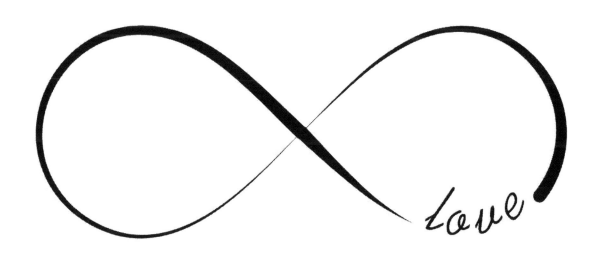

KEEP YOUR CIRCLES LOVING
Let's Connect

Rob & Jacq

🌐 TheLettersofGratitude.com

👍 TheLettersofGratitude

✉️ TheLettersofGratitude@gmail.com

🐦 TheLOGTweets

Dani Nir-McGrath

🌐 SpiritualJunkies.com

👍 ShopSpiritualJunkies

Pat Armitstead

🌐 Joyology.co.nz

✉️ If you would like to connect with any of the other contributors, please send your note to Rob & Jacq and they will be sure to pass it along

ABOUT THE AUTHORS

Rob and Jacq are passionate about making a positive impact in the world. In 2012, they traded their careers for a life of travel and adventure. Their nomadic lifestyle affords them time to follow their ever evolving passions and embrace new cultural perspectives. Their journey led them to the calling of *The Book of Love.* It is through writing, gratitude, and acts of love that they aspire to create change. They are immensely grateful for everything that has led to this publication.

62560846R10123